An Angel on My Shoulder

MY FIRST 100 YEARS
A MEMOIR

**JERRY ROSENBLUM
AND JACK NEWORTH**

An Angel on My Shoulder

MY FIRST 100 YEARS
A MEMOIR

**JERRY ROSENBLUM
AND JACK NEWORTH**

DORRANCE
PUBLISHING CO
EST. 1920
PITTSBURGH, PENNSYLVANIA 15238

Dorrance Publishing Co
585 Alpha Drive
Suite 103
Pittsburgh, PA 15238
Visit our website at www.dorrancebookstore.com

ISBN: 978-1-6442-6154-5
ISBN: 978-1-6442-6131-6

DEDICATION

I dedicate this memoir to my late mother, Nettie, who lived to be 102. (Born in Russia in 1897, if she had passed away 6 weeks later, she would have lived in 3 centuries.) She gave me so much love and wisdom throughout her long life and also nurtured my passions for story telling and music.

I also dedicate this to my late brother, Arthur. At 47, Artie was tragically taken from us way too early. But his children, grandchildren and even great-grandchildren, make up my extended family that has encouraged me, along with many friends, to put these oral history stories down on paper.

And lastly, I dedicate this memoir to one of the best friends I've been lucky enough to ever have, Katie Miller who's 28 but is wise by decades beyond her years. Katie and I first met when she volunteered to help seniors with their computers at my apartment building. Even though I don't have a computer we became, as she would put it, BFFs (best friends forever.)

Among so many things Katie has done for me, she set up an Instagram account (@Jerry_Rosenblum) for me because she wanted others her age to know. (That's so flattering, I'm blushing as I type.) She also had put 14 videos of me singing. (At YouTube "Jerry Rosenblum Sings.") I'll end by simply saying, Katie's friendship has truly added years to my life and life to my years.

I started this memoir at 87 and I'm finishing it at 98, all in the hope that maybe it will give you a few laughs and, more importantly, that it somehow inspires you to lead the fullest and most rewarding life possible.

TABLE OF CONTENTS

FOREWORD XI

1: A.O.C. AND ME (2020) 3

2: A BOY GROWS IN BROOKLYN (1922) 7

3: LUCKY LINDY SHOCKED THE WORLD (1927) 11

4: THE GREAT DEPRESSION, PLUS MY FLY WAS OPEN (1929) 15

5: SNEAKING INTO THE MOVIES (1933) 17

6: THE BOY IS FORCED TO GROW UP IN A HURRY (1934) 19

7: MY FIRST JOB AND WAS MY FACE RED (1935) 21

8: A VISIT FROM MY GUARDIAN ANGEL? (1936) 25

9: THE NICEST PRESENT A KID COULD EVER GET (1937) 27

10: MY HEART WAS BROKEN, BUT NOT BY A GIRL (1937) 29

11: BEWARE OF THE BOUNCING BALL (1938) 31

12: WELLES FREAKED OUT MR. WEINER (1938) 33

13: I KNEW LARRY TISCH BEFORE HE WAS LAURENCE (1939) 37

14: MISTAKEN IDENTITY COULD HAVE GOTTEN ME KILLED (1939) 41

15: ONE O'CLOCK JUMP ENDED OUR LIFE OF CRIME (1939) 43

16: VOILA, THE FRENCH SAILOR GOT ALL THE GIRLS (1940) 47

17: PEARL HARBOR ENDED OUR INNOCENCE (1941) 49

18: ALL ABOARD, BUT WAIT, DON'T LEAVE WITHOUT ME! (1943) 53

19: DESTINATION HONOLULU, UNLESS WE GET TORPEDOED (1943) 57

20: CANDID CAMERA, HAWAIIAN STYLE (1944) 61

21: RACISM WAS ALIVE AND NOT SWELL (1943) 65

22: WE THOUGHT FOR SURE WE WERE GONERS (1944) 69

23: DADDY NEEDS A NEW PAIR OF SHOES (1945) 71

24: WHOEVER SAID "WAR IS HELL..." (1944-1945) 73

25: PEACE AT LAST, THANK GOD! (1945) 75

26: WILL THE REAL PUSSY ROSENHEIM STAND UP? (1945) 77

27: THE POLICE AND I CRACKED THE CASE (1947) 81

28: THE ICEBOX CHRISTMAS (1947) 83

29: THE TRUE STORY BEHIND TV GUIDE (1948) 87

30: RUN EVERYBODY, THE STORE IS ON FIRE (1949) 89

31: FEELING SORRY FOR MYSELF ALMOST TURNED DEADLY (1949) 91

32: NO GOOD DEED GOES UNPUNISHED (1950) 93

33: MOM COULD BE A REGULAR HEDDA HOPPER (1957) 95

34: ANYBODY GOT CHANGE FOR A GRAND? (1953) 97

35: MY GANGSTER "FRIEND" MEETS A BAD END (1954) 99

36: TURNS OUT A FEW CUSTOMERS WERE JAILBIRDS (1947-1957) 101

37: MY "CAREER"" IN THE NUMBERS RACKET (1957) 103

38: THE REGISTERED LETTER (1959) 105

39: MOM MEETS JFK... SORT OF (1960) 107

40: A VACATION THAT WOUND UP FEELING LIKE WORK (1961) 109

41: CHATTING WITH A PULITZER PRIZE WINNER (1962) 111

42: I DIDN'T GO IN SPACE, BUT I KNEW TWO WHO DID (1962 & 1969) . . . 113

43: GO WEST YOUNG MAN, ONLY I WASN'T THAT YOUNG (1963) 115

44: SAVING A SINKING SHIP (1963) 119

45: CESAR: ET TU, JERRY? (1964) 121

46: THE BEST LUCK IS WHAT YOU MAKE YOURSELF (1965) 125

47: THE PERNICIOUS PERKS OF POLITICIANS (1968) 127

48: MY VACATION CROSSED PATHS WITH HISTORY (1968) 129

49: GETTING A PINK SLIP STINKS! (1968) 131

50: TURN ON THE BUBBLE MACHINE (1969) 133

51: WHAT THE WELL DRESSED MURDERER SHOULD WEAR (1971) 135

52: EXCUSE ME, BUT SHOULDN'T YOU BE IN JAIL? (1972) 139

53: I FELT LIKE NOAH, ONLY WETTER (1972). 141

54: THE CLOSEST I CAME TO AN OSCAR (1972) 143

55: NOT ENOUGH TIME WITH ARTIE (1974). 145

ADDITIONAL PHOTOGRAPHS 147

56: AFTER SIX SHOWS IN A ROW, I WAS ALL "MERVED" OUT (1975). . . . 163

57: COMEDIAN FLIP WILSON GOT THE LAST LAUGH (1975). 165

58: A DRUNK WITH A GUN, A SCARY COMBINATION (1975) 167

59: BING CROSBY WAS GOING MY WAY (1976). 169

60: MOM MURDERS 'EM AT THE GONG SHOW (1976). 171

61: ONE DEGREE OF SEPARATION FROM
THE HILLSIDE STRANGLERS (1976) 173

62: OLD BLUE EYES WAS NOT FOND OF MOTOR MOUTH (1977) 175

63: JESSE OWENS WAS AS NICE AS HE WAS GIFTED (1978) 177

64: "UNCLE MILTY" COULD ALSO BE "UNCLE MEANIE" (1978). 179

65: THE CRIMINAL RETURNS TO THE SCENE OF THE CRIME (1979) 181

66: THEY CALLED HIM MR. TIBBS (1962, 1979 & 2009). 183

67: LIFE IS BUT A CIRCLE (1978) 185

68: J.F.K. GAVE SOME GOOD ADVICE (1979). 187

69: THE HIGH CLASS HOOKER & THE LEATHER JACKET (1979) 189

70: A MIDDLE EAST CRISIS IN CENTURY CITY (1970 & 1980) 191

71: WHEN THE GOING GETS TOUGH, HIT THE ROLODEX (1978) 193

72: HE WALKED THE LINE, BUT IT WASN'T EASY (1978). 197

73: I SHOULDA BEEN A HOLLYWOOD TALENT SCOUT (1979) 201

74: THE DAY I SOLD 1000 PAIR OF SOCKS (1980) 205

75: WHEN ONE DOOR CLOSES,
DON'T LET IT HIT YOU IN THE BUTT (1980) 207

76: MY MOBSTER CUSTOMER GOT WHACKED (1983) 209

77: THE MILLION DOLLAR MERMAID (1984) 213

78: DENNIS WAS ENGAGED TO LIZ FOR...1 MINUTE! (1985) 217

79: MY NEIGHBOR, THE KID TV STAR (1987). 221

80: RUMORS TO THE CONTRARY, OLD AGE CAN BE FUN (1991-2019) . . 225

81: STREISAND, GOULD, ELVIS AND MOM (1994) 229

82: ALI, HE WAS THE GREATEST (1974 & 1997) 233

83: MOM TURNS 100! (1997) 235

84: IN LOS ANGELES A PARKING SPOT IS TO DIE FOR…
ALMOST! (1998) 239

85: CUT TO THE CHASE! (2001) 241

86: WHAT A MAN WILL DO FOR LOVE (2004) 245

87: THE PARKING VALET NEEDED LASIK SURGERY (2005). 247

88: SINGING FOR MY SUPPER (2005) 251

89: MY DELIGHTFUL DEBUT IN DOO-WOP (2007). 253

90: DYAN CANNON AND I "CHAT" ABOUT CARY (2011). 257

91: IS 98 TOO LATE FOR ME IN ADVERTISING? (2012) 261

92: "YOU'RE IN LUCK, THERE'S ONE TICKET LEFT" (2014) 263

93: MY NERVOUS RETURN TO THEATER PALISADES (2014) 265

94: A FRIENDSHIP FOR THE AGES (2015) 267

95: MY HILARY CLINTON "AFFAIR" (2015) 271

96: THOMAS WOLFE WAS WRONG (2018) 275

97: LITTLE MISS SUNSHINE IS ALL GROWN UP (2019) 279

98: DID I FINALLY MEET MY GUARDIAN ANGEL? (2019) 283

EPILOGUE 287

IN 50 YEARS IN MEN'S CLOTHING,
SOME OF JERRY'S MORE FAMOUS CUSTOMERS. 291

ACKNOWLEDGMENTS. 297

FOREWORD

I first talked to Jerry Rosenblum in 2008 when he was 87-years-young. (Trust me, in his case the cliche is incredibly fitting.) As a regular reader of my weekly column in the Santa Monica Daily Press, he had gotten my phone number from a mutual friend. With boyish enthusiasm, he wondered if I might take a look at a memoir he had just completed.

I was diplomatically explaining that I was "kinda busy" when Jerry mentioned he had been in the men's clothing business for 50 years. As it happens, my late father had owned a men's store for 30 years. So, somehow, I felt compelled to meet Jerry. Eleven years later, I'm eternally thankful that I did.

A dapper dresser, Jerry was also intelligent, well-informed and had a truly unbelievable memory. (Still does!) After our cordial meeting during which Jerry told some stories and jokes, I read his memoir over the weekend. Albeit reluctantly, I had to tell him it needed work. I explained it was a series of amusing anecdotes but without an overall story line. He understood immediately and even agreed. Well, at 98, Jerry finally finished his book. How's that for persistence?

"Angel," is Jerry's first book. (However, knock wood, Jerry's hoping to write "Angel on My Shoulder, Part II, to celebrate his 100th birthday!)

As the memoir reveals, at age 7, Jerry's life went from idyllic to tragic. Following the Great Depression of 1929 and the untimely death of his father, at 12, Jerry was forced to become the "man of the house." For solace, he imagined he had a guardian angel looking out for him. (Real or imagined, on occasion she "appears" in the book.)

As an incredibly resourceful preteen, Jerry often had three jobs, working diligently to support his mother and younger brother. During the following 58 years, Jerry was unemployed for a total of two weeks. But since retiring at age 70, he began living the childhood he didn't really have. He did so by traveling the world via luxury cruises and "doing something fun every day."

Remarkably, Jerry's thankful for the work ethic he was forced to adopt at such a young age. "The Depression taught me not to feel sorry for yourself because somebody always has it worse than you. Be grateful for what you have, rather than lament about what you don't."

(By the way, the existence of Jerry's "guardian angel" is "resolved" in the very last chapter.)

Uplifting at its core, "Angel" is often funny and emotionally moving and filled with valuable lessons we learn from Jerry's remarkable life. (There are 98 fast-paced chapters, one for each year of his life.) So it is, if you're reading this in a store, I hope you'll buy it and you too will be thankful you got to "meet" Jerry. If you're at home and just now starting "Angel," I predict you're in for a real treat.

Jack Neworth,
Santa Monica Daily Press

An Angel on My Shoulder

MY FIRST 100 YEARS

A MEMOIR

CHAPTER 1

A.O.C. AND ME (2020)

In my long life I have lived through the Great Depression, WWII and "The Gong Show." (My 80-year-old mother was a contestant.) Given my longevity, I've acquired some perspective. So let me share the following "Only in America" story of someone I admire enormously.

A year and a half ago, Alexandria Ocasio-Cortez, 28, was waiting tables in a New York city taco bar, which is hard and honest work. However, serving tacos is not typically a springboard to becoming the youngest Congresswoman in history. She's also the most famous freshman member of Congress in almost 200 years. Former President John Quincy Adams was elected to Congress in 1830. (And no, I wasn't there. I'm old, but not that old.)

How did I come to meet AOC? Though I've lived in Los Angeles since 1963, I was born and raised in Brooklyn and sometimes miss the "action" of NYC. As a result, I still closely follow the goings on in my "home town."

So it was that I noticed Alexandria when she was running for the Democratic nomination for Congress against Joe Crowley, a 10-term incumbent in the 14th District, which covers part of the Bronx and portions of Queens. I saw a brilliant TV campaign ad of hers entitled "The Courage To Change." (Given the odds against her, AOC had me at "Courage.")

The video followed her during a typical, harried day for a working-class woman just trying to stay above water. Yet, I didn't think she had a chance against an incumbent who often ran unopposed and, in this primary, would outspend her $10 to $1.

But she won and won big. Not only was I shocked, so was she! On TV the night of the election, I saw her at her headquarters as results were coming in. An aide insisted AOC look at the tote board and her jaw dropped in disbelief. I could read her lips, "Oh, my God, we're going to win!"

Being an amateur songwriter and singer, I immediately began composing a song extolling AOC's abundant virtues. The melody that ran through my head was a tango "Adiós Muchachos," which was written in 1927. Here's the opening stanza of my "version" but remember to keep the tango beat in your head:

> "Alexandria Ocasio-Cortez, if you're elected, here's what's expected/
> Lower cost on our medications, and that you'll fight to get us free edu-
> cation/With your vitality and vibrant personality, you can do it, so just
> hop to it."

My young friend, Katie, whom I mentioned in the dedication, used her iPhone to record me singing the song. Then she posted it on AOC's Instagram. To my utter delight, AOC posted a wonderful "thank you, Jerry" video. I was totally stunned.

**Congresswoman Alexandria Ocasio-Cortez and Jerry 12/21/2019
(Photo courtesy Sheila Laffey)**

In May, 2019, I wrote another song for Congresswoman Ocasio-Cortez, entitled, "A.O.C. Are Her Initials" which she posted and I got 1,100,000 views in 3 hours!

Katie then opened an Instagram account for me and AOC became one of my "followers," of which I have 22,100. But I don't want to get ahead of myself.

As seemingly the whole world took notice, AOC easily won the general election in November 2018 and has been a lightning rod ever since. In April she was on the cover of Time Magazine, captioned, "The Phenom."

Meanwhile, as I write this, four days before Christmas 2019, I met AOC in person! It was one of the happiest days of my life and I describe the meeting in detail in the epilogue. To give you an idea of her charisma, her very first speech from Congress, a powerful rebuke of the government shutdown, was broadcast on CSPAN and put on their Twitter feed. It was so brilliant and passionate it broke all records for the number of views in CSPAN history.

I have a strong feeling this remarkable young woman could be a POTUS one day. I pray that with extraordinary luck, I could see her Inauguration. But, if I'm no longer in this world, I only hope wherever I am, they have good cable reception.

But now, dear reader, I'm now going to take you on a trip down memory lane way back to the beginning of my life history, which, to some degree, coincides with the country's history. With each chapter we will get closer to the present. So buckle up and don't forget to bring your funny bone.

CHAPTER 2

A BOY GROWS IN BROOKLYN (1922)

In 1945, Betty Smith wrote a classic American novel, "A Tree Grows in Brooklyn." Semi-autobiographical, it's an inspiring story of an impoverished adolescent girl, Mary Frances (Francie) Nolan and her immigrant family living in a Brooklyn tenement, during the early 20th century. It's a tale of hope and the American dream. I, too, was born in Brooklyn in the early 20th century, and I suppose you can say I shared Francie's hopes and dreams.

I was born in 1922 and I still remember the address of the apartment building we lived in, 252 South 4th Street. The reason I remember is because at 3-years old, when I said the address, my mother's friends got such a kick out of it.

The era would become known as "The Roaring 20's," given that label because of the loud, exciting and exuberant events of the times. WWI, which was sold as "the war to end all wars," was over there was genuine hope for a long lasting peace. Wasn't to be but people didn't know it and the country's mood was very upbeat.

There were wild, free-spirited parties being held in cities such as New York, Chicago and New Orleans, characterized by excess and opulence. Oddly enough, the opulence was in part a reaction to prohibition laws, which, in 1920, outlawed the sale and consumption of alcohol. Prohibition even affected my father.

My dad, Morris ("Mike") Rosenblum was a cab driver in Manhattan and he knew where to "hack," meaning he knew where the customers would be,. He always made note when a luxury ship was landing at the docks or where drunken patrons at various speakeasies would need a ride home. (FFor serious mobsters, on occasion, my dad actually transported cases of alcohol in his cab to the speakeasies.)

My mother, Nettie Rubin, met my father in 1920. In those days, if a woman wasn't married by 23, she worried she would become an "old maid," or "spinster." So my mother "knocked off" two years from her age when she first started dating my father. It was just a small fib but many years later, it backfired. When she turned 65 and applied for Social Security, to her chagrin, they told her to come back in two years. (She only had herself to blame but boy, was she peeved.)

My young life seemed idyllic. My mother and father loved me dearly and we had moved from Williamsburg to Flatbush, the latter being a much nicer neighborhood and nearer to the ocean. I remember being so happy that when I was about 3 and my mother held my hand as we walked, I apparently stuck out my chest proudly. At 3, I'm not sure what I had done that I was so proud about. But apparently the butcher said, "Here comes little Jack Dempsey." And that story was told often.

When I was 5, my mother gave birth to my brother, Arthur. I loved having a baby brother, whom I would always take care of. When he was old enough to walk on the sidewalk, I always held Artie's hand. (As I write this, Artie's son, Mark, and daughter, Heidi, are coming this week to visit me from Florida. How lucky am I?)

My parents came from Russia at a young age, but didn't meet until many years later in the U.S. When Dad arrived, like millions of others, he had to quickly find work, learn the language and try to assimilate. His older brother, Jacob ("Jake") was already here and owned a small tuxedo rental business.

Uncle Jake and Aunt Jenny lived in the Bronx and rented dad a room in their four-room apartment. Mutual friends introduced my mother Nettie, to my dad and he fell in love immediately. And why not? Nettie was very attractive, funny, had a great singing voice and was the life of the party. (If I'm a "ham," with my singing, story telling and jokes, it's definitely from her DNA.)

Outgoing and attractive as she was, it wasn't surprising that my mother had two other admirers besides my father. But my dad had persistence. (Inasmuch as it's taken me 10 years to write and re-write this memoir, apparently I inherited that DNA as well.)

So my parents wound up marrying about six months after they met. Mom was a woman who knew how to save money and in a few years Dad was able to buy his own taxi-cab. Until then, he had been driving someone else's and was taking home only part of the proceeds. Mom once told me she saved ten thousand dollars because dad was doing so well. Back in the 20's that was a respectable sum. (Actually, it doesn't sound so bad, now!)

Dad was a World War I veteran. He had volunteered and the army, seeing that he was a cab driver, assigned him to drive ambulances on the battlefields of France. He never talked about it, but I can only imagine the horrific sights he saw in battle.

In those days, there was a considerable amount of anti-semitism in the armed services. But dad didn't take guff from anybody. He was built like a prize fighter and could handle himself. Dad received an honorable discharge in 1918 and I still have the papers in a bank vault here, in Santa Monica. Just to look at it gives me great pride.

Taken without my permission.

As a boy I liked school, had lots of friends and I loved sports, especially baseball. My young buddies and I would play stick ball with a rubber ball in the streets. We'd chop off the broom part of a broomstick for a bat and we were ready to go. One day, however, I hit a ball so high and far, it landed a block away on the roof of a Jewish synagogue.

The balls were 10 cents so I decided to walk to the temple and ask the rabbi if he'd let me go on the roof to retrieve my ball. Apparently I caught the rabbi in a bad mood because he chased me out of the temple. (For all I know the ball may still be up there, though at a minimum I'd say it's probably lost its bounce.)

While my life felt idyllic, in a matter of years, two major events, would change my world forever and force me to face challenges I couldn't have imagined.

CHAPTER 3

LUCKY LINDY SHOCKED THE WORLD (1927)

When I was 5, much of the planet, was experiencing exciting events. Young as I was, I obviously didn't understand the significance, but I could still tell excitement was in the air.

In 1927, the World Series Champion New York Yankees may have had the best team in baseball history. They had Babe Ruth whose home run hitting changed the game and first baseman, Lou Gehrig, who would become known as the "Iron Horse" because he played in 2,130 straight games.

The Yankees batting order was so lethal they were known as "Murder's Row" and struck fear in the hearts of opposing pitchers. There was only one problem. I was a Dodger fan! After all, we lived in Brooklyn.

As for going to baseball games, for a nickel, my friends and I could take the subway to Ebbets Field to see a Dodger-Giant doubleheader for 55 cents as we sat in the bleachers. My mother would make me a couple of sandwiches, salami and eggs, on a seeded roll that she would put in a brown bag. And a Pepsi-Cola was only a nickel. Suffice it to say, in spring and summer, I was in heaven.

Also in 1927, an amazing event occurred that shook the world. On May 20, a handsome, blond 24-year-old pilot named Charles Lindbergh climbed into his silver plane, the Spirit of St. Louis, with five sandwiches in a paper bag and a St. Christopher medal in his pocket. Thirty-three hours and 30 minutes later, he landed in Paris and stepped from the cockpit into a crowd of 150,000 cheering people.

Lindbergh's solo, non stop transatlantic flight would be the first step in bringing the world closer and stimulated further development of the relatively new commercial airlines. Because of his heroic feat, Lindbergh became an instant international hero. In 1974, when he died at 72, his reported net worth was $20 million. ($100 million in today's dollars.)

Following his historic flight, Lindbergh was given the nickname "Lucky Lindy" and there was even a dance that was attributed to him, the "Lindy Hop." Streets and entire towns had been named after the world famous pioneer/hero Lindbergh but he would eventually have a spectacular fall from grace.

Meanwhile, "Lucky Lindy's" luck ran out on March 1, 1932, when Charles Lindbergh III, the 20-month-old son of Lindbergh and his wife, Anne Morrow Lindbergh, was abducted from his home in East Amwell, New Jersey. I was ten at the time and saw the newspaper headlines, read the stories and heard about the kidnapping on the radio as the country was obsessed with every detail.

The Lindbergh's discovered a ransom note in their son's empty room demanding $50,000. The kidnapper used a ladder to climb to the open second-floor window and left muddy footprints in the room. The Lindberghs were inundated by offers of assistance, even from Al Capone who was in prison.

In September 1934, a marked bill from the ransom turned up. It was traced back to a German immigrant carpenter, Bruno Hauptmann. When his home was searched, detectives found some of the Lindbergh ransom money.

In January, 1935, in what was described as the "trial of the century," (almost 60 years before O.J. Simpson's "trial of the century") Hauptmann was convicted of murder in the 1st degree. In April, 1936 he was electrocuted. Both events had the country riveted to their radios and following the details in newspapers, which had banner headlines almost daily.

In the aftermath, kidnapping was made a federal offense. The Lindbergh kidnapping affected all of us kids and left us cautious, if not downright scared. As for Lindy's "fall," it began in 1938, when he aligned himself with the "America First" campaign and "eugenics." which advocated that some races of humans were superior to others.

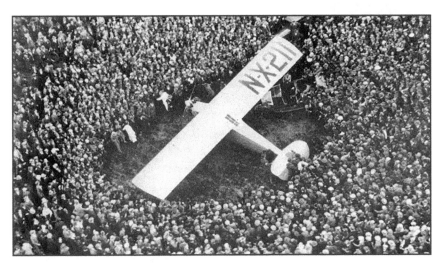

150,000 jubilant Frenchmen greeted Lindbergh.

Lindbergh also visited Hitler on numerous occasions, spoke highly of the German Air Force and, in October 1938, received the Nazi Service Cross of the German Eagle. When WWII broke out is when Lindbergh was perceived by many to have been racist and unpatriotic. Lindbergh wanted to join the military but FDR and Winston Churchill had not forgiven him. His reputation was a far cry from the young man who had captivated the world.

1927 was a dramatic year in my young life but what would happen in 1929, and especially the years that followed, would affect me in a far more profound and frightening way.

CHAPTER 4

THE GREAT DEPRESSION, PLUS MY FLY WAS OPEN (1929)

At age 6, I started first grade at P.S. 153 and life was great. However, on October 29, 1929, the stock market crashed, though at my age and living in Brooklyn, it didn't really impact me. Not yet.

Unfortunately for my father and our family, the taxi business was no longer thriving. Very few people could afford to ride in cabs in those days. Dad worked twelve and fourteen hours a day in all kinds of weather in order to bring home enough money to keep a roof over our heads and food on the table. And he had to work exclusively at nights.

In actuality, the Depression had a deep impact on me as I rarely got to see Dad because he was asleep when I went off to school and at work when I got home and had dinner. I remember wishing I could have what almost all my friends had, fathers who were around more. The fact, ninety years later, that I really never got to know my father, is still one of the few regrets in my life.

As I got slightly older other aspects of the Depression became more obvious and worrisome to me. In our living room, we had a big, beautiful Majestic radio. It was more like a piece of furniture than just a radio. It was about 4 feet high and 3 feet wide.

I remember listening with my mother to FDR giving his "fireside chats" that were designed to comfort the country. He was such an excellent communicator, it was as though he was in the living room with us. (My brother Artie was only 2, so he didn't exactly listen with us, though often he'd be playing in the room as we sat riveted by FDR's every word.)

In one fireside chat, he carefully explained the banking problems in language easily understood. He outlined why he had closed the banks for a week to stop the "run on the banks" where people withdrew their funds so feverishly it threatened what was left of our economic stability.

He further explained how he would fix the system and, in a comforting tone, encouraged people to take their cash out from under their mattress and re-deposit it into the banks. And amazingly, the following Monday, when the banks re-opened, people waited in long lines to put their money back into the banks, even though there wasn't yet FDIC (Federal Deposit Insurance Corporation) that insured accounts up to a certain limit.

It's hard to imagine that kind of trust a country could have in their president. In that aspect, I wish we could turn the clock back. Some of FDR's "fireside chats" are on YouTube. I highly recommend you listen to some to get a feel for the era.

And now for the above mentioned "open fly" incident, which honestly, at my pre-adolescent age, was more mortifying than the Great Depression. It took place in my classroom where Mrs. Gordon was my teacher.

I was a pretty obedient youngster and tried to stay out of mischief. One day while sitting in her classroom, Mrs. Gordon said in a rather stern and loud voice, "Jerome, come up to my desk." It was so loud the whole class heard. I immediately thought to myself, "What have I done?" I could tell my classmates were wondering the same thing. I immediately got up and walked very slowly to her desk as she had requested.

"Jerome," she said in a voice that, unfortunately, could be heard by the other kids, "your fly is open!" Keep in mind that back then they didn't have zippers in the fly, they had buttons and buttonholes. My face turned beet red from embarrassment. I quickly glanced downward and, sure enough, she was right. Why hadn't she told me in private? Or at least not so everyone in the class could hear. Sheesh.

Though I was quite popular, the whole class had a good laugh. If there had been a hole in the floor, I gladly would have crawled in and disappeared. Maybe forever, or at least until the next school year. Exasperating things, because of my nervousness and embarrassment, I fumbled to get my fly closed. The laughter only increased.

Finally, I got the fly closed and sat back down in my seat. To my utter relief, by then, the laughter had subsided and we continued with our school work. I could hardly wait for the school bell to ring so I could go home and pretend it hadn't happened.

Believe me, for years afterwards, I was overly careful to check that my fly was always closed. (In case you're wondering, I just checked. It's closed.)

CHAPTER 5

SNEAKING INTO THE MOVIES (1933)

In 1933, when I was eleven (a mere 86 years ago) we lived in Brighton Beach in Brooklyn. I palled around with kids my age whom I knew from P.S. 225. I used to love to see a good movie and still do to this day. (As it happens, I even take a film class at the Emeritus College in Santa Monica.)

But, in those Depression years, money was very tight and we couldn't afford to step up to the box office and pay a 25 or 35-cent admission. So we devised what we thought was a clever, albeit a little risky, way to get into the movie theater without paying any money. Here's what we did.

A brand new movie theater, The Oceana, had recently opened. (By the way, the theater is still there!) This week I'm talking about, Fred Astaire and Ginger Rogers were starring in a new musical and we were all anxious to see it. Admission was thirty-five cents so seven of us chipped in a nickel each. Six kids would climb up a fire escape on the side of the building.

The seventh kid would buy a ticket at the box office and worriedly explain to the cashier that his little brother was inside the theater and had been there for at least four hours. His mother was understandably concerned and sent him, the older brother, to look for his kid brother and bring him home. While he was willing to buy a ticket to get it in, he told the cashier he would be right out.

Without fail, the now worried cashier would take the 35 cents with the understanding that the worried boy would hopefully return very soon with his missing brother in tow. Our pal would repeat the same story to the ticket taker who wouldn't tear the ticket in half. Keep in mind if this were today, with so much random crime, it's possible the cashier might have called police or security and our buddy would have been in the hottest of water. But these were infinitely more innocent times.

Once inside the theater, our pal would walk up the stairs to the balcony. Quiet as a church mouse, he'd open the side door for us, and six kids would tip-toe into the theater. The last kid in would leave the door slightly ajar.

Then our buddy would exit the theater and tell the cashier his younger brother wasn't there and could he have his money back. The cashiers were always happy to do so and usually told our friend something like that she hoped his brother was at a toy store or something and would be home soon. Sometimes we'd be a little guilty how worried the cashier and ticket takers would get.

With his money refunded, our friend would go outside. Making sure nobody was watching, he would saunter casually toward the side of the building. Again, looking over his shoulder, he'd proceed to climb the fire escape to the open door and quietly enter the theater and shut it behind him. We always would manage to find seats together.

My favorite actors of the era were: James Cagney, Humphrey Bogart, Pat O'Brien, Errol Flynn, Tyrone Power, Frederic March, and John Garfield. I also very much liked the following actresses: Bette Davis, Joan Crawford, Jean Harlow, Marlene Dietrich, Greta Garbo, Vivian Leigh, Joan Fontaine and Olivia de Havilland. (Who, as I edit this in 2019, is 106 years old! God Bless her.)

When we got a little older, we devised a little more sophisticated and less taxing way to get inside the theater without paying. We would show up just at the end of a movie, when people were exiting the theater. When the doors opened and people began leaving the theater, we would make it appear that we were leaving, too.

But, instead of walking out with the group, we would casually walk into the theater backwards. I don't remember which kid thought of the idea originally but it was quite brilliant. I say that because it was surprisingly easy and we never had a problem. Actually, I take that back.

One time, the other kids got in, but the theater Assistant Manager, a big guy by the way, grabbed my arm. And he was pretty furious as he demanded my name. I was quite scared, but I knew enough not to give him my real name, so I made one up.

"My name is Jerry Smolofsky." I blurted out nervously. "Spell it!" he said. Unfortunately, I didn't know how to spell so, stalling for time, I went very slowly. "S..M..O..L..O.." I went so slowly, that the Assistant Manager got even madder. "Get the hell out of here and don't ever come back!" (I couldn't get out of there fast enough.)

I have some advice for any kids reading this. Don't ever try to sneak in anywhere. But, if you do, at least know how to spell the phony last name you're going to give.

CHAPTER 6

THE BOY IS FORCED TO GROW UP IN A HURRY (1934)

This chapter will probably be the toughest for me to write in the whole book. Hopefully, you'll soon understand why.

Dad taught me the value of hard work.

It was November 12, 1934, at the height of the Depression and I remember it was a very cold day. I was 12 and Artie was 7. There was a knock at the door about 7 P.M. It was two policemen who asked if Mom was home, which she was.

When Mom came to the door they told her, "Morris Rosenblum had died of a massive heart attack." (My dad smoked 2 packs of Murad Turkish cigarettes daily but in those days no one knew smoking was so dangerous.) The police explained they tried to save Dad, but to no avail. I was so devastated, I actually thought I was going to faint. One thing's for sure, I shall never forget that day because it changed my life forever.

My father was gone and, sad to say, I hardly knew him. Ever since the market crashed in 1929, he worked nights and slept during the day. I, of course, was in school during the day and, when I came home from school, Dad was getting ready to go to work. Suffice it to say, my father's passing was an emotional shock to me, my mother and brother. But it was also a financial shock.

Fortunately, for my family, FDR was president. I say that because in 1932, within days of taking office, he had set up the New Deal that included a new welfare system because so many millions of people were out of work.

Before the Great Depression, new immigrants were able to depend on relatives for help when they arrived. And also there was so much new industrialization and farm work that welfare was not really needed. Anyone who wanted to, it seemed, could find a job. During the Depression at least 25% of the country was out of a job.

Mom had two brothers, Hyman and Gabriel. Hyman, a woolen jobber, was married with two children, and Gabriel worked at a millinery factory making ladies' hats. Unfortunately for them, and us, both businesses were adversely affected by the Depression and neither brother could help us financially.

My poor mother was grieving but she had to take care of two young boys. And I felt I had to take care of her, which I would do for the rest of her life.

After the funeral, family and friends came to our apartment to commiserate. My Aunt Mildred said something to me that resonated so deeply, it changed the entire direction of my young life. "Well, Jerry, now you're the head of the family." It hit me right then. At 12, I was going to learn to make the best of the cards I was dealt, a motto I still live by.

On that cold dark day in November, 1934, when my dad passed, I realized I was going to have to do all I could to help financially support my mother and kid brother. But being so young and at the height of the Great Depression, how was I going to do it?

CHAPTER 7

MY FIRST JOB AND WAS MY FACE RED (1935)

My father had left us some life insurance but the money didn't last long. My mother did the best she could but soon we were falling behind on the bills, including the rent. She tried to keep the bad news away from her children, but she couldn't hide that we were being evicted. As I write this in 2019, eighty-five years later, I still feel very sad when I think about it and can remember the shame we felt.

We were able to move in with some cousins not far away but it was only temporary. When they picked us up, I remember being in the back seat as we drove away from my apartment with my mother and younger brother. I looked out the back window for the last time, and I saw our furniture piled up on the sidewalk. Tears flowed down my cheeks but I didn't want my mother to see as I knew how hard this was on her, too.

Thank God for my family and millions like us that FDR was elected because President Hoover had done nothing to help the poor. He and the GOP were of the view that the "market" would make the necessary corrections that ultimately would restore prosperity. I remember going to the movies while Hoover was still president and when the newsreel showed footage of him the entire audience would boo at the screen.

But large business interests in the U.S. were worried FDR was going to transfer wealth from the uber rich to the poor. In 1933 there was even a fascist coup attempted headed by enormously wealthy business interests. They tried to get General Smedly Butler, the most decorated General in the history of the Marines to lead the coup because he was so popular with the troops. But Butler never intended to cooperate and ultimately exposed the coup. (Google "FDR coup attempt.")

FDR explained to the rich elites that if he failed to restore the country's economy the masses might revolt and come to the homes of the super wealthy seeking revenge. He tried to convince them he was their best and last hope.

In any event, FDR set up a system of "relief" for families like mine. Never giving up for a second, my mother applied for General Relief and fairly soon, thank God, we were able to get an apartment of our own. The rent was $47 a month. It was in a rundown neighborhood and the apartment was so small I couldn't believe my eyes. But it was a roof over our head and we were back on our feet.

So many of us were so grateful for FDR it was common in my friends' homes to see a framed photo of him hanging in the living room. What most of us didn't know was that FDR had polio since he was 39 and was in a wheel chair. But the press voluntarily agreed to never take a photo of him in that state and we didn't realize when he gave speeches from a podium he was propped up with the use of braces.

Ever since my Aunt had told me that now I was "the man of the house," I never forgot my responsibility. Even though I went to school full time and always had homework, I was determined to get a job. But New York had child labor laws which forbade a child under the age of 14 from working. But I didn't let it stop me.

The idea I came up with was to go to every drug store in my neighborhood and those close by and ask if I could make deliveries for them. This wasn't against the law because I was doing it on my own and wouldn't be on their payroll. At least that's what I convinced myself and fortunately it never became an issue.

If the drug stores didn't have any deliveries, I'd ask if they had any fliers they wanted put under the doors of apartments in the neighborhood, which was a common practice to promote a big sale or a grand opening. I could get a few dollars for a job like that.

And during the winter, I'd borrow the snow shovel from our building janitor and shovel people's driveways, for which I could also get a few dollars. (Though when I'd come home hours later I'd have built up a ravenous appetite!)

I guess I was a natural born salesman, because I convinced a handful of drug store owners to give me a chance. As it evolved, each druggist would give me a dime for each delivery, though it was never a formal agreement. And, sure enough, when I would make the deliveries, I would invariably get a tip from the customer. Often, it was a dime, but sometimes it would be a quarter. As hard as I hustled, to my delight, it started to add up.

This went on for two years. Mr. Weiner, the owner of one of drug stores, was so impressed with my work habits, that exactly on my 14th birthday he offered me a steady after school job. The hours were 3 p.m. to closing at 9 p.m., with an hour off for supper. (I only lived 2 blocks away so I would rush home for dinner and, after eating, would rush back to work.)

In the summer, when school was out, I even finagled a second job, this at the Brighton Beach Baths, a private beach club. The club had swimming pools, tennis, basketball, handball and volleyball courts and a solarium where men would sit around wearing towels and play poker.

The room was quite hot and the men would drink lots of water as they played cards. One of them would often say, "Deal me out, I"m going to fill up the water pitcher and go across the street and get us some sandwiches." A light went off in my head!

Given my young age, it was quite bold of me to volunteer my services to be their "gofer." But, to my delight, the group was impressed with my moxie. "What the hell," one of them said, "Okay, kid, you've got yourself a job." So, for about 3 hours a day, I became the group's gopher, getting water, sandwiches and cigarettes. And often, when one the players would win a big hand, as he put aside a few dollars he'd say, "This is for the kid."

Believe it or not, many days I would get an extra $5 or more that way and in the course of the week, that accumulated pretty fast. My mother was very proud of my enterprising nature and also grateful for the money. (When I graduated high school, I passed along the Beach Club "gopher" job to my kid brother, so you could say the gig stayed in the family.)

At the drug store I started at $6 a week and worked my way up to $12 a week over the course of the next four years. Keep in mind, when I'd be working, most of my friends were playing in the school yard. But I never felt sorry for myself, as I was glad I was able to earn money for my family.

I pretty much became indispensable to Mr. Weiner. Even one time when the window dresser didn't show up, I volunteered to take his job for that day, and I created a presentable display. Mr. Weiner was very impressed. And, my printing skills were so good that Mr. Weiner, who didn't have a typewriter, would have me print the directions to a medication on a label and then I'd paste that label on the bottle.

Mr. Weiner also let me handle the cash register allowing me to ring up sales. But, maybe about once a year, I felt as though he was testing my honesty. On these occasions, I'd find a dollar bill on the floor next to the counter as though a customer had dropped it. I'd pick up the bill, which I suppose I could have put in my pocket, but instead I notified Mr. Weiner.

Taking the bill, Mr. Weiner would thank me for my honesty. I was pretty sure that had been a test that I passed with flying colors, which was no big deal to me because I was an honest kid. (If you don't count sneaking into the movies.)

So everything was great until one day, not long after Mr. Weiner let me work behind the cash register, a grouchy man approached the counter impatiently, "Three rubber bands," he said gruffly. I thought it was an odd request but I gave him 3 rubber bands, much to his displeasure. "Kid, get the pharmacist out here, pronto." he barked.

I started working at Weiner Drug in 1936 for a whopping $1 a day.

Mr. Weiner heard the unhappy customer and came right out. He opened a drawer, pulled out a small box and handed it to the customer who paid and left hurriedly like he had something important to do. I was completely confused.

Apparently Mr. Weiner felt it was time for me to learn something about the birds and bees. Showing me the open drawer, he said, "This is where we keep the 'rubber goods.'" He winked, and then it dawned on me that the customer's request for "three rubber bands" was code for three condoms, which were in the box Mr. Weiner sold the customer. My face was quite red.

Now, as they say in movie scripts, flash forward twenty years when I was 34, far from naive and impatient myself. You see I was late for a "hot date," and I hope you'll forgive me, needed some "rubber bands."

As I drove to pick up my date I saw a drug store still open, though the lights were going off and they were about to close. I rushed in and, to my surprise, the pharmacist and her two employees were all women. I was so embarrassed somehow, I couldn't bring myself to ask for what I needed so I turned around and started to leave.

"Wait," the female pharmacist, said very authoritatively, "we have what you want. Right here on the counter." I was flustered. "Sir," she said boldly, "this is a very progressive drug store." How did she know what I wanted? Was it that obvious? I guess it was. In any event, "rubber bands" in hand, I left the store as the three women were chuckling to themselves.

CHAPTER 8

A VISIT FROM MY GUARDIAN ANGEL?
(1936)

On a nice summer Sunday afternoon when I was off work and 14 at the time, my friends and I went to Brighton Beach Baths. We had a regular routine. We would play a few games of handball, work up a good sweat and head for the ocean to swim. Back then, there were two rafts anchored in the ocean about fifty yards from the shore.

Before I go any further, I have a brief confession. When my father passed away and I was 12, it radically changed my life. Seemingly overnight, I went from being just a kid, to being the man of the house. As a result, I didn't really have a typical childhood.

I also didn't have time or outlets to grieve the loss of my father. I couldn't go to my mother because she was so overcome herself. What I think I did, perhaps subconsciously, is I invented the notion that an angel in heaven came to earth and was looking out for me. (Curiously, I've never shared this with anyone until now.)

Back to my story about the rafts at Brighton Beach, which were about twenty-five yards away from each other. We swam out to one, climbed aboard and sunbathed. After fifteen minutes or so, someone suggested we play "follow the leader." (Given what almost happened it could have been called "follow the idiot." Anyway, it began when the self-appointed leader dove off the raft and swam to the other raft, all under water.

I had never smoked and by playing lots of handball and basketball, I had a healthy pair of lungs. Also, I had done lot of underwater swimming. Well, when my turn came, I dove into the water, got down about seven or eight feet and started swimming to the other raft. It was pretty murky down there at that depth and when I was sure I had reached the other raft, I began to surface. What happened next was very frightening, to say the least.

I apparently had overshot the mark and came up under the raft. By then, I had very little breath left. It's been said when someone is about to die their whole life flashes in front of them.

Well, that's what I was experiencing at that moment. No fun, trust me! (In one of his early 1960's stand-up routine, Woody Allen joked about his life flashing in front of him, until he realized it wasn't his life.)

In utter desperation, I flailed around, down there, at the eight-foot depth and just when I thought that I was a goner, at the last second, either luck, fate or an angel intervened, because I managed to get out from under the raft. Well, by then, all my friends were peering down, looking to see where I was. They sensed something was terribly wrong and were about to dive into the water hoping to find me.

I climbed aboard the raft, much to the relief of my friends and myself. Thoroughly grateful to be alive, I nonetheless had a throbbing headache for about three hours until finally things got slowly back to normal.

At my current age, I don't have swimming to rafts out on the ocean on my current schedule. That said, even at 98, I wouldn't mind some snorkeling in Hawaii. As for do I still believe in an angel on my shoulder? If you promise not to skip forward, I will tell you I answer that question in the very last chapter.

CHAPTER 9

THE NICEST PRESENT A KID COULD EVER GET (1937)

The Great Depression caused enormous hardship for my family and for tens of millions of families across America. It was a dismal time for many who just wanted basic human needs i.e. a job, food and shelter.

While many people were understandably concerned with how they'd survive, there were also many who looked with compassion at the those worse off than they were. Even at a young age, I felt this way. I learned to never complain about what I didn't have but rather appreciate what I did. It was a valuable lesson I carried throughout the rest of my life.

It's probably difficult for people today to imagine the scope of the Depression. As much as 25% of the population was unemployed and who knows how many more were underemployed. And many, many hard-working people, who had put their savings in the banks, discovered to their horror that their money was gone forever.

Not long ago I read a book about the famous UCLA basketball coach, John Wooden, who was about to marry his high school sweetheart, Nellie Riley. They went to the bank to draw out their combined life savings to buy a car and put a down payment on a house. But the bank had failed. They were completely wiped out just as they were to start their life together.

Wooden's basketball teams would win a record 10 National Collegiate Championships. And yet, with all that success, he never forgot that horrific experience of losing his life savings. He also never once asked for a raise for fear that, odd as it sounds, he might lose his job. Go figure.

The Great Depression shaped my life, too. I saw downtrodden people standing in lines at soup kitchens. Tent cities sprouted up all over the country. From my family's experience I knew that very bad things could happen to very good people. So I learned to not judge others and respect and have compassion for people who were trying their best to get by.

After the Great Depression and my father's passing, every free moment away from school, it seemed, I was busy working to earn money for my family. But, on rare occasions, some Sundays, I would be able to rejoin my friends in playing baseball. The only problem was my baseball glove had long ago worn out and, with my family's dire economic straits, I couldn't dare buy a new one.

So I would play with my friends and when the other team was at bat, I would borrow one of the guys' mitts to play in the field. I had once been the unofficial captain of the team and was still very well liked, but it was embarrassing to be without my own mitt.

A few Sunday's later, I showed up at the sandlot and my friends were all excited for some mysterious reason. I would soon find out as moments later, they gave me a present all wrapped up. I eagerly unwrapped the gift to discover it was a brand new, beautiful leather mitt. I got all choked up seeing that and each one my friends gave me a hug. As I said above, I will never forget that day and their loving gesture. (And honestly, I also loved that mitt!)

So, these days, if I ever find myself discouraged with humanity and begin judging others, all I have to do is remember that baseball glove my friends bought me eighty-five years ago. It can still bring to my eyes, tears of joy.

CHAPTER 10

MY HEART WAS BROKEN, BUT NOT BY A GIRL (1937)

You could say this chapter is about my heart being broken. And no, it wasn't over a girl, though I had my share of puppy love heartbreaks. Actually, this heartbreak involved playing sports or not being able to. I shall explain.

Let me begin by saying, as a boy, and even well into adulthood, I was a very good athlete and loved sports. If it involved a ball, I was good at it. What I was best at, was handball, because I was fast and determined and just seemed to have a gift for it. And when I was a kid, handball was a very popular sport, especially in the big cities.

In fact, handball was an Olympic sport at the Summer Games in Berlin in 1936. For reasons that aren't entirely clear, it was dropped for the next 40 years but has been back ever since 1976. Don't get me wrong, I certainly wasn't an Olympic level handballer, but, at the same time, I was pretty damn good. I was so good in fact our high school coach eagerly recruited me to play for the school team. But first, let me note that our high school basketball team won the City Championship that year and I had dreams our handball team might be able to do the same with me leading the charge.

Unfortunately, because of my family's economic situation, I worked 30 hours a week. With school and homework, well, I just couldn't make the time to practice with the team. Our coach was very disappointed, while I was beyond disappointed, I was heart broken.

There was some joy for me regarding sports, however, albeit fleeting. At my old grade school, P.S. 225, there was a school playground. On Sundays, a regular group of grownups used to play softball there. There were some very good players, guys in their mid to late twenties. I remember the pitcher who wore glasses and had a wickedly fast under-arm pitch.

Well, right about that time, the Hearst Newspaper organization decided to run a contest to see who had the best softball team in the USA. The name of the local team from Brighton Beach was known as the Worsted Yarns. Where or how they got that name from I'll never know. It refers to wool is about all I can tell you.

After many weeks, through the process of elimination, the Worsted Yarns had won every one of their games. It reached a point where were going to play the team from Chicago for the championship of the entire country in Yankee Stadium! And I was invited to attend, which I dearly looked forward to.

I had never been to Yankee Stadium in my life. First of all, I was a Brooklyn Dodger fan, so the Yankees were kind of the enemy. Also, just getting to the Bronx was a huge trip from Brighton Beach.

And keep in mind, the only time the Yankees in the American League and the Dodgers in the National League, would meet would be in the World Series. Their first Series meeting was 1941, which was a few years away. (In 2019, as I edit this, a great many baseball fans are hoping for for a Yankee-Dodger World Series for this season.)

On the day of the big softball championship, when I first entered Yankee Stadium, it was impressive to say the least. I could just imagine all the great sports moments that had been played in this legendary stadium. As for Babe Ruth, he retired in 1935 so there was no chance of seeing him. But it felt like a World Series to me. Most importantly, our team won and in front of a pretty huge crowd, reportedly well over 10,000 fans. I had a wonderful time watching and rooting our guys to victory as I wolfed down way too many hot dogs and Cracker Jacks.

Understandably I slept contentedly that night. Almost. I kept dreaming that I was the star of our high school handball team and we won the City Championship. Only the Championship was played in Yankee Stadium,which made no sense. I knew I shouldn't have eaten those last two hot dogs.

CHAPTER 11

BEWARE OF THE BOUNCING BALL
(1938)

In 1938. I was 16 and my brother Arthur was 11. Our family lived in an attic apartment in an old, wood-framed house on Coney Island Avenue in Brooklyn. Nearby stood a large, old, wood-framed house and it had a huge back yard with an old barn that was guarded by a rather large dog.

My brother had been bouncing a rubber ball on his side of the fence when it took an unexpected bounce over the fence separating the two properties. And, wouldn't you know, the ball came to rest at the feet of this large dog. Well, Arthur knew enough not to hop the fence because that dog would surely go after him. So, as far as he was concerned, it was a lost ball.

We didn't give it any more thought until one day, not long after the incident, an article appeared in the New York Daily News that caught my attention. It seems that the family that lived in the large frame house was blackmailing a CEO of a corporation that was listed on the New York Stock Exchange. I became fascinated by the details.

The executive's last name was Costa. However, it seems that Mr. Costa wasn't always Mr. Costa. You see he had a prison record in his past and had changed his name from Musica to Costa. The family that was blackmailing him was named Brandino. Well, when all this was found out, the police were all over the property. And, lo and behold, they found a still inside the barn. No doubt that is why the large dog was there. They were selling bootleg liquor!

As I said, all this took place in 1938. Now, let's push the fast forward button forty years later to 1978. I was managing the men's clothing store in the Century Plaza Hotel in Century City, Los Angeles. At this particular time the McKesson Company was having their annual convention at the hotel. And it just happened to be that the McKesson Company was the name of the company whose CEO in 1938 was Mr. Costa.

Well, who comes into the store? None other than the man who was now CEO of the McKesson Company, a very large pharmaceutical company. Waiting on him, I found a pair of slacks he liked, which he eagerly took into the dressing room.

Call me a bit weird (and many have) but, even though forty years had gone by, I remembered the blackmailing incident as if it had happened the day before. When the CEO of McKesson came out of the dressing room, I told him about the episode with the Brandinos.

He couldn't get over the fact that, so many years later, I could describe the events in such detail. He told me that when this had taken place he was working as a lowly shipping clerk at McKesson and he, as all of the company would learn from the newspaper accounts, knew of the blackmail.

How did this "coincidence," connecting events separated by forty years, happen? And why would they happen so often in my life as I will share in this memoir? I don't know the answer. On the other hand, if they hadn't happened and often connected up decades later, this book would be a heckuva lot shorter.

CHAPTER 12

WELLES FREAKED OUT MR. WEINER
(1938)

Here's another vignette about Weiner's Drugstore. I never really found out what possessed Mr. Weiner, but fortunately it never came up again and we just moved on like nothing happened, which was fine by me. And yet, here I am writing about it a mere 81 years later.

The year was 1938 and I was 16. One evening, the late actor/director Orson Welles, who, unbelievably to me, was only 6+ years older than I was, put much of America into sheer panic. Let me explain how and how it affected me, and even more so, Mr. Weiner.

You see, despite his youth, Welles had a highly successful radio program called The Mercury Theater. My boss, pharmacist Mr. Weiner, stayed in the rear of the store most of the time filling prescriptions and always seemed to have the radio on.

For those too young to know of Welles, he would go on to be among the great geniuses of film. His first movie, "Citizen Kane," released in 1941, is considered by many as the greatest American movie of all-time. (Is that all?)

Mr. Weiner and his wife lived in an apartment above the store. She would bring his lunch and dinner to the store and he'd eat in the backroom while listening to the radio.

Mr. Weiner was listening to Welles' Mercury Theater. Suddenly, in the middle of the program, a voice came over the radio: "May we have your attention! We have just had a bulletin handed to us, reporting that creatures, evidently from another planet, have landed in New Jersey. We have reason to believe they may have come from Mars."

The reporter sounded very convincing at first, but soon I recognized the voice to be one of the actors who was a regular player in other Mercury Theater broadcasts. Entertaining as it was, I quickly surmised this was all a hoax. What was to follow was Welles' radio version of H.G. Wells book "War of the Worlds," first published in 1898. So you could say it was Welles doing Wells. (If you're groaning now, sorry about that.)

Normally an intelligent and very reserved man, Mr. Weiner seemed to believe the invasion from Mars was actually happening. There was zero doubt in my mind, however, that it was just an entertainment radio drama. For example, I quickly recognized Joseph's Cotten's voice, who, ironically, because of the uproar that followed Welles' "War of the Worlds" was actually rewarded because of his newly-found notoriety with an impressive contract from RKO Pictures.

As I look back, I guess Mr. Weiner was tired and overworked perhaps. One thing was for sure, he got very scared by what he was hearing. One way I could tell is when I kept trying to explain to him it was just a radio show, he kinda snapped and yelled at me to "shut up," which he had never even come close to doing before. In fact, even my own father and mother had never yelled at me like that. While I knew I was right, I also realized at that moment that being right could possibly cost me my job. And, even at 16, given my family's economic situation, I couldn't jeopardize my job.

Rather frantically, Mr. Weiner ran out of the store and began looking up into the darkness, I assumed to see if men from Mars were landing in Flatbush. I couldn't help but think humorously to myself if Martians were out there, what was poor Mr. Weiner going to do? Sell them some Pepto-Bismol? (Do Martians even get upset stomachs?)

So I returned to re-stocking the shelves as the broadcast continued in the background. As time went by, I jokingly wondered if the Martians had possibly captured Mr. Weiner, and if so, would they be my new bosses? I was only getting $1 a day, so maybe I could ask the Martians for a raise.

About fifteen minutes later, an exhausted Mr. Weiner came into the store but he didn't seem rattled, just exhausted. He looked like the poster boy for "Having a Bad Day." Albeit timidly, I asked if everything was okay. He said, yes and that I could go home early, which I did.

The following day, newspapers from coast to coast reported on the turmoil that Welles' show had caused as police switchboards were flooded. In Newark, more than twenty families rushed out of their houses with wet handkerchiefs and towels over their faces to flee from what they believed was to be a gas raid. .

Throughout New York, families left their residences, some to flee to near-by parks. Thousands of persons called the police, newspapers and radio stations in cities across the United States, and even Canada, seeking advice on protective measures against the Martians.

Reportedly in Providence, Rhode Island, "weeping and hysterical people" swamped the Providence Journal with calls asking for more details of the "massacre." In Pittsburgh, the Associated Press reported, a man returned home in the middle of the broadcast and found his wife with a bottle of poison in her hand, saying, "I'd rather die this way than like that."

The next day Welles was forced to speak at a press conference to apologize to listeners who had taken the broadcast seriously. To me he seemed thoroughly puzzled that people could have possibly thought it was real. (Both the apology and the broadcast itself are on YouTube.)

One day, a little more than three years after the "War of the Worlds" broadcast, I found myself standing directly next to Welles waiting for the traffic light to change at Avenue of the Americas and 50th Street in Manhattan. "Citizen Kane" has recently come out and Welles was even more famous than he was before. In person, he was also even more handsome and exceedingly intelligent looking.

Just as I was getting up the nerve to say hello to Welles, and maybe tell him about me and Mr. Weiner on the night of the radio broadcast, the light changed. (Thank God, because I would have sounded so foolish.)

I started to follow Welles in the crosswalk, however at the other side of the intersection a beautiful woman gave him a hug and they walked off. (No, for movie buffs, it wasn't Rita Hayworth whom he married in 1943 and divorced in 1947.)

The only other time I saw Welles was in 1953. By then I was a successful clothing salesman at Kallen's Clothes in Manhattan, and I saw Welles, looking thoroughly aloof, coming down the steps at St. Patrick's Cathedral. Only by this time, he must have weighed 300 pounds and was wearing a big black cape that covered his girth. I had a feeling the last thing he would want to do was talk "The War of the Worlds" through the eyes of a then 16-year-old.

The funny thing was that numerous celebrities came into Kallen's, many of whom I waited on. And it had actually crossed my mind that Welles might one day come in. I hate to say this, but at his weight, we wouldn't have had any suits that would have fit him. Then again, among the many challenges Welles would face in his absolutely fascinating life, I imagine having to get his suits made to order, wasn't at the top of the list.

CHAPTER 13

I KNEW LARRY TISCH BEFORE HE WAS LAURENCE (1939)

When people ask me how I've lived such a long and rewarding life, I usually answer, "Be grateful," and "play the cards you are dealt." I'll try to explain both, hoping I'm not repeating myself. (Only in this case, I think it's so important it might be permissible.)

I'm talking about being grateful for what you have and making the best of it, rather than dwelling on what you don't have.

Sometimes friends joke, "Jerry's grateful he's so grateful." I laugh but I think it's true. Okay, enough of my personal philosophy or I fear I'll put you all asleep.

One last bit of gratitude is, knock wood, that, I still have a great memory, even at 98. Though it's 90 years ago, I can remember the names of my teachers and the kids I went to school with. One I will describe below.

Laurence (Larry) Tisch was a highly successful businessman, Wall Street investor and billionaire when it was a more exclusive club than it seems today. He was the CEO of CBS from 1986 to 1995 and part owner of the Loew's Corporation. But by then he had long ago become "Laurence." When I knew him he was just "Larry."

In fact, Larry and I lived on the same street, though about a mile apart. He lived in the ritzy neighborhood and we lived in the working class section, but it was still the same street. Funny how a mile of the same street can represent two such different worlds.

I've dated this chapter "1939" because Larry and I went to James Madison High School in Brooklyn during that year. Larry was exceptionally bright but the next year he was transferred by his parents to a high school that prepared him for a career as an engineer. And you just knew he was going to amount to something really big.

I graduated from Madison and eventually, I ended up in the men's retail clothing business after World War II. In 1950, Wolfgang Kallen, my boss, took a week's vacation at the Grand Hotel in the Berkshire Mountains. When he came back to the store, he told me that the two gentlemen who owned the hotel were coming into the store with their father to buy him a suit. He wanted me to wait on them.

So it was, to my complete surprise, in walks Larry Tisch with his brother, Preston, and their father. Even though about fifteen years had passed, Larry and I still recognized each other and we even exchanged "long time no see" hugs.

As I would learn, after WWII, Larry's father gave his two sons one hundred thousand dollars each to invest in a business of their choosing. (A pretty tidy sum in those days. Actually still a pretty tidy sum.)

The two brothers purchased the Grand Hotel. They were good at trimming costs and soon had the hotel turning a profit. Next, they purchased Laurel in the Pines, another hotel in Lakewood, New Jersey, where people would go for treatment if they had an arthritic condition. This hotel also became successful.

As they now had two hotels making money, they purchased the Traymore, an old hotel on the Boardwalk in Atlantic City. They refurbished the Traymore and it too became successful. (Are you seeing a pattern, here?) Next, they built a high-rise hotel in Times Square called the Americana and another hotel in San Juan, Puerto Rico also called the Americana.

Next, the Tisch's started buying stock in Loews Corporation, a company listed on the New York Stock Exchange. Loews owned a chain of movie theaters, though some were not doing well because of competition from TV. But not to worry.

Eventually, the Tisch's became the majority stockholders in Loews and determined the defunct movie theater locations would be more profitable if hotels were located on the sites instead. The Summit Hotel is an example that comes to mind. I'm sure there were others, too.

I had moved to Santa Monica in 1963 when it was a small, sleepy beach town. Almost all the "hotels" and motels were mom and pop operations. That is, until 1989, when a big New York city corporation built a big hotel overlooking the ocean that seemed to change our city forever. (Some say for the better, others sarcastically call Santa Monica "Dubai by the Sea.") What corporation did this? Loew's headed by my old school mate, Larry Tisch, who was now Laurence Tisch.

No, I didn't run into Larry. But, as it happens, four years ago, I stayed at the Loew's Montreal. I had taken a plane to Dulles Airport, and then took a prop plane to Montreal. There I would board a cruise ship that would go down the Atlantic Ocean on its way to Key West, Florida where I would visit my extended family in Boca Raton.

I was very hungry that night I arrived in Montreal and felt like a cheeseburger so I went into the ultra-swanky dining room. However, as I glanced at the menu I was more than a little taken aback as it seemed even a hamburger was $50. (It had a French name so I guess that's why it was so expensive!) The helpful waiter, in all sincerity, suggested that right around the corner was a McDonald's.

After Larry became president of CBS and his picture was on the cover of Time magazine, I sent him a congratulatory letter. I reminded him that we went to high school together and that I had sold he and brother a suit for their father many years ago.

To my total surprise, Larry sent me a thank-you note that I've saved, together with the Time magazine. Lawrence Tisch passed away about two years ago and his brother Preston passed shortly after. Both widows are alive and their sons are running the business, and what a business it is.

Speaking of their sons, as I contemplated writing this book, and had finished this chapter, I sent it to Larry's son, James. Again, to my surprise, I heard back. He was delighted to read about his father when he was teenager. He even suggested that, when I came to New York, we would have lunch. You could say I was on cloud nine.

But, when I visited New York, James was too busy to keep our appointment and the luncheon date never took place. Not that I can blame him. To be totally honest, if I was a billionaire, I might be too busy to have lunch with me either. (Then again, if I was that rich at least I could afford that $50 hamburger.)

CHAPTER 14

MISTAKEN IDENTITY COULD HAVE GOTTEN ME KILLED (1939)

In 1939, I was in high school and we lived on Coney Island Avenue near Neck Road, Brooklyn. One day during summer, I was coming back from visiting a friend. I was wearing a pair of slacks and a shirt, walking along, heading home and minding my own business. The neighborhood consisted of private homes set back from the street about forty feet, and each had a front lawn.

Suddenly, I heard the screech of brakes and a police car turns the corner and stops right next to me. Guns drawn, two cops get out and shout, "Hands up!" It just about paralyzed me. One of the cops ordered me, Get in the car, now!" I went from paralysis to my knees knocking, literally. Stammering, I replied, "I haven't done anything."

Though I tried to hide it, my whole body was shaking. One moment I was walking contentedly on a summer afternoon and the next moment, I'm staring at guns pointed at me by two shouting cops. It all happened so fast.

Just then, I heard a woman yelling from her front porch, "That's not him!" The cops put their revolvers back in their holsters. One walked to the woman, while the other made sure I didn't move.

Even from where I was, I could hear the woman explaining that her six-year-old daughter had been playing in the alley. That's when a man, wearing the same color slack and same color shirt as I had on, tried to molest her daughter. She frantically called the police station which was only four blocks away, so they rushed over.

Given the police almost put an innocent person in the car, and did so with guns pointing at me, do you think they apologized? Hardly. They got back into the car and probably circled the neighborhood looking for the guy.

To think that if not for that woman on the porch, I could have been shot, or, at a minimum, hauled to the police station. When I protested that I hadn't done anything, one of the cops barked, "Tell it to the sergeant," as though everybody says they're innocent, which I suppose many do.

The vast, vast majority of people in prison are guilty of the crimes they were charged with. That said, there are a frightening number of inmates you see and read about that are, in fact, innocent. It happens all too often.

If not for that woman, God knows what would have happened to me. We've all read about innocent men and women being in prison for ten or twenty years because of mistaken identity. There are even examples of people being executed for a murder they didn't commit. (In 2014, CNN presented "Death Row Stories," with Robert Redford as one of the executive producers as the series documents real life examples of people almost executed by mistake.)

I'm certainly not an expert in the criminal justice system and what, if any changes, need to be made. I can only say this, however, what happened to me was seventy years ago. And, in writing this, I relived the entire frightening event all over again.

Lastly, I try to end these stories with something amusing or at least a cliffhanger of some sort. As you just read, thankfully, I was not put in the police car. In fact, in my entire life I've never been in a police car, which, hopefully, almost all of you might be able to say the same thing.

In my case, however, I did eventually wind up in a police car. And I was 96 at the time. You'll just have to keep reading to find out the "lurid" details. (Remember, no skipping forward in the book.)

CHAPTER 15

ONE O'CLOCK JUMP ENDED OUR LIFE OF CRIME (1939)

In an earlier chapter, I wrote about my friends and me sneaking into the movies when we were quite young. My closest of those friends was Marty Shapiro. We both loved movies and I still do to this day. (Thankfully, I long ago gave up sneaking in!) As I think back, though, I must confess that the thrill of sneaking in added my enjoyment of the film itself.

So it was that when the 1939 World's Fair came to New York City, Marty and I put our heads together and planned how we were going to attend this major world event for free. To be fair (no pun intended) to us "gate crashers" the tickets were $5 and at that time I only made $10 for an entire week's work.

Frankly, despite the magnitude of the event, it actually wasn't that difficult to sneak in. For starters, we wore all black clothing (instead of Men in Black, we were Boys in Black) and planned the "break in" at night. We merely climbed a 10 foot fence (this was long long before the concept of Donald Trump's wall.) And minutes later, voila, we were among the "paying customers."

The highlights of the Fair included the "World of Tomorrow" where they featured what the American kitchen would look like in the 1950's with dish washers, fancy refrigerators and they exhibited a device for the future, a thing called "television," (That ruled the world until a thing called the I-phone.)

But, to be totally honest, the main draw for Marty and me was Billy Rose's Aquacade, which was set around the biggest pool I'd ever seen. The production featured female synchronized swimming numbers and a high diving platform.

Marty and I were mesmerized, especially when Rose introduced the "Long Stemmed Beauties," beautiful models in swimsuits who were breathtaking and talented. Then they changed into colorful Gay 90's costumes and they sang "Oh You Beautiful Doll."

I know in this "Me Too" era, this may not be all that politically correct, but their beauty was something to behold. Today I see beautiful women and I'm stunned to find they're wearing jeans with holes in them! (I still can't believe they buy them that way!)

After our success at the World's Fair Marty, and I were pretty confident. Our next "caper" was the ritzy Manhattan Beach Club where the crème de la crème did their summer gallivanting in the Atlantic Ocean and did their sun bathing on the warm sand. Our plan required that we had to scale a wall to drop ourselves down on top of the steel lockers which were just inside the perimeter of the club.

The wall was approximately 10 feet high. What we had to do was get a running start and jump as high we could to grasp our fingers on the ledge. At the time there was a dance craze spawned by a very popular song by Count Basie called the "One O'clock Jump." That's what Marty and I called our jumping feat.

It often took a number of leaps but somehow we always managed to scale that wall. That left us on top of the lockers and we simply dropped ourselves down to the ground. Then we looked for an empty locker. We had our bathing suits under our pants so we merely took our pants and shirts and put them into the locker. We brought our own cheap combination lock, locked the locker, and we were done! We did this many times without a single hiccup.

Like we were hoi polloi, we'd swim in the pool and the ocean; we'd play handball and watch Class A and Class B exhibition handball players compete for trophies. There was also world class entertainment. There was Benny Goodman with his featured drummer, Gene Krupa, and the big band who performed. Milton Berle was the featured comedian. We took it all in like paying customers who belonged there. (Not for long, but I'm getting ahead of myself.)

We also saw Rudy Vallee and his orchestra, the Connecticut Yankees. Vallee was a heart throb to young women and many consider him the first "crooner" to make the female gender swoon. His act also featured the famed and beautiful "singing actress," Alice Faye, who captivated the men in the audience. Marty and I certainly had many memorable afternoons like this, all because of our One O'clock Jump. That is until one fateful day when you could say the music stopped.

After another successful One O'Clock Jump, we had an enjoyable day at the club. It was late in the afternoon and we were ready to leave to attend a dance party with male and female friends, often held in the basement of friend's parents' home. We went to our locker to change into our street clothes only to discover the lock was gone. The door was wide open and the locker was empty!

Completely confused, we stood there with our mouths open but not for long. Moments later we were approached by a barrel chested security guard you wouldn't want to argue with. "We are going to teach you juvenile delinquents a lesson once and for all," he bellowed.

We were frozen in fear and nearly speechless as he explained our clothes were confiscated and "You're not getting 'em back, wise guys." "But how do we get home?" we asked, almost in tears. "That's your problem, punks. Now scram before I call the coppers."

In shock, we hurried off the property in only our bathing suits and sneakers. Luckily, we both had carfare (a nickel!) in our trunks which was enough to get us home on the trolley car. But the embarrassment of riding all that way in a pair of wet bathing trunks, well, we felt like were naked as people stared at us like we were bums or weirdos. Put it this way, we avoided making eye contact for the entire trolley car trip and the eight block walk back home. (In our bathing suits no less!) Both seemed like they took forever.

When the gruff security guard said he was going to teach us a lesson, that's what he did. Our days of sneaking into places came to an abrupt halt. (For more, go to YouTube "Count Basie One O'Clock Jump." Also "1939 World's Fair.")

CHAPTER 16

VOILA, THE FRENCH SAILOR GOT ALL THE GIRLS (1940)

This chapter occurred one Sunday in the spring of 1940. Three of my friends and I were enjoying refreshments in an ice cream parlor located on Kings Highway between East 17th and East 18th in Brooklyn. It was about 1 p.m. and just then, we all noticed a French sailor walking alone and heading toward us. On his cap was the word "Richelieu," the name of the largest battleship in the French Navy.

As we would learn, the ship was docked in New York and the sailor was on shore leave. One of my friends spoke a little French, having studied it in high school. So when the sailor was passing us, my friend said, "Bon jour." Keep in mind, France was already engaged in World War II against Germany. They were and still are our longest running ally, so we were already disposed to be friendly to this fellow.

The sailor smiled and said, "Parlez vous francais?" Then my friend asked, in French, whether he spoke English. He did but just a little. At that point, the sailor explained in broken English that the Richelieu was docked in the Brooklyn Navy Yard for repair work. He was given an eight-hour pass and was exploring his new surroundings. He had taken a subway and had decided, for whatever reason, to get off when it stopped at the Kings Highway Station.

One of my buddies had just recently become the proud owner of a Chevrolet convertible. He suggested that we all chip in a dollar and take our new found friend to Coney Island. We wanted to treat him to an ice cream cone, hot dogs at Nathan's, let him have a ride on the Cyclone and pay his way into the freak show on Surf Avenue.

We piled into the Chevy and drove to Coney Island where the Frenchman had a great time and said to us, "I will remember this for the rest of my life." That made us feel terrific. Now it was time to take him back to the spot where we had started.

As we were driving along Surf Avenue in the open convertible, he asked the driver to please stop the car. You see, he noticed a very attractive young lady walking all by herself and he wanted to meet her. We stopped and he walked over to her and they had a very brief conversation. I noticed he wrote something down in a little black book...her phone number!

When he got back into the car, he told us that he had asked her what her name was and she answered, "Yetta." He immediately told her he was changing her name to Yvette. This guy was a smooth operator and we could see he wasn't bashful.

We rode back to where we had started. In thanking us profusely for the great time we had shown him, I remember his parting words were, "Tomorrow I bring ze whole ship." Oh, brother, what had we started?

Charming as he was, and ally or no ally, we could see this French romeo could wind up being a pain in the butt. Plus he'd hog all the girls!

CHAPTER 17

PEARL HARBOR ENDED OUR
INNOCENCE (1941)

Probably everyone in America above the age of 5, can remember when a huge tragedy took place and how it affected the whole country and left the nation walking around in a daze. What I'm referring to is JFK's assassination on 11/22/1963. I loved JFK so much, I still feel pain when I think of that awful event. Because of the mystery surrounding the assassination that still exists, and the love the country had for JFK, I'm not sure we've ever fully recovered. But that's for another story at another time.

The most recent such event, I suppose would be 9/11/2001, when the World Trade Center were brought down by terrorists who hijacked and then flew huge jets into the towers. But for now, I want to write about another such day, December 7, 1941, said by FDR in a powerful and memorable speech to Congress and the nation as, "A day that will live in infamy."

First let me set the stage. After I graduated high school I managed to get a job working as a stock boy and deliveryman in a very busy liquor store in downtown Manhattan. That happened in early 1940. From age 14 to 18 I had worked for Mr. Weiner at his drug store.

I had learned so much from Mr. Weiner and had gone from a young boy to a young adult, but it was time for a change. At the liquor store I started out at $18 a week and, while it may not sound like it, it was definitely a step up. That was how it was on December 7, 1941. I was 19 soon to be 20.

That afternoon, along with my buddy from the liquor store, Jack Sachs and his fiancee, a very cute girl aptly named Pearl, I was on a double date. Actually, for me it was a blind date with a 17-year-old girl named Ruthie Bell, with whom I had been set up. When I knocked on the door, Ruthie answered and, in all honesty, she was the prettiest female I had ever seen in person up to that point in my life.

Ruthie was petite, blond, blue-eyed and had an outgoing, upbeat personality. To say I was immediately smitten was an understatement. So it was the four of us drove in Jack's car with the radio playing the Tommy Dorsey orchestra with Frank Sinatra doing the singing. We had lunch at Child's restaurant in Times Square and then we went to the Strand Theater nearby to see the movie, "They Died With Their Boots On," starring Errol Flynn and Olivia de Havilland. We were all having a great time and I was head over heels about Ruthie. And I sensed she liked me, too.

Everything was terrific until, right before the movie started, a full Colonel in the army, and in uniform, came on stage and made a very serious announcement. One, that you could say shaped the rest of my life and probably the life of everyone in the audience. He said that if there were any people in the military in the audience, that they should immediately report to their base.

To our complete shock we learned Japanese bombers had attacked the American base at Pearl Harbor causing enormous damage to our fleet and enormous loss of life. "We are engaged in a war!" he said somberly. He didn't exactly say, "And now enjoy the movie." Actually a hush came over the crowd and, we decided under the circumstances, we ought to leave and take Ruthie home.

Ironically, none of us had ever heard of Pearl Harbor before. And little could I imagine that in 18 months I'd be working as a machinist at Ford Island Naval Air Station in Pearl Harbor, but, again, I don't want to get ahead of myself.

As I walked Ruthie to the door, we agreed to have another date soon. In fact, we would go out a total of 5 times. I thought Ruthie might be the girl for me, but soon a girlfriend of hers, told me that Ruthie, having come from a poor family, was intent on marrying a man who was born into money or had a bright future or both. I certainly wasn't born into money and frankly I didn't know what my future would be. I was a bit heartbroken but I understood what Ruthie was looking for and I wished her the best as she did me.

Meanwhile, following the attack at Pearl Harbor, the country was in complete panic. On December 8th, FDR addressed Congress and they voted to declare war against Japan. Three days later, Germany declared war against the U.S. and we responded in kind. Suddenly we were in World War II in a huge way. It's hard to describe how much the entire world changed in 96 hours.

Soon the entire planet would be engaged in the biggest war in history costing the most money and more importantly, costing the most loss of life in history. Suddenly, as kids today might say, "Things got very real!" One thing was for sure, our days of "innocence" were over.

Within 24 hours I received a call from one of my best friends, Marty Shapiro, or as we called him "Soupy." (Even though I'd known Soupy since I was six, for the life of me, I can't remember how he got that nickname.) You might recall I wrote about Marty and I sneaking into the World's Fair in 1936 and our ill-fated crashing the Manhattan Beach Club only to get caught and wind up going home on the trolley in only our swim suits.

But this was the day after Pearl Harbor. Marty told me he had just started to work for a company at 388 Broadway called Premier Tool and Instruments. This company was producing bullet dyes and supplying another company called Remington Arms. With the war on, their business was booming. (Pun intended.)

Evidently, Premier was looking for men and I could start at fifty cents an hour. (Believe it or not, that was a considerable pay increase for me.) I told Marty I had no experience working in a machine shop. He said they would teach me what to do.

An important factor for me was that Premier was considered a defense plant and therefore my draft status could be changed to 2-B. (In addition, because I was the sole provider for my mother and brother, I was double protected from being drafted, at least for a while.)

The work at Premier was monotonous but the pay was good and, of course, I got to see Marty every day at lunch. Because of the job my mother's financial situation was stabilized and my younger brother, Artie was doing well in school. But this "opportunity" that knocked on my door, so to speak, would eventually lead to another huge "life changing" step.

First, I want to share that during the war, if you were a man and not in the service, there was a certain stigma that perhaps you weren't patriotic. I would run into women I knew from the neighborhood, mothers and grandmothers, whose sons and grandsons were fighting overseas. And they might be a little suspicious it seemed when talking to me as why wasn't I in the service. I could certainly understand their point of view. I mention this in light of the "opportunity" that was soon coming my way.

After about a year at Premier, I received a letter from another old friend from the neighborhood, Al Glassman, who was working at as a machinist at the Navy Yard in, of all places, Pearl Harbor. (Between Marty and Al, two neighborhood friends, I might not be alive today. I'll try to briefly explain.)

Marty helped get me the job at Premier. And now Al was telling me about civilian jobs opening up in Pearl Harbor that I'd be qualified for, that would pay double what I was making. And equally as important, without both those friends and the jobs they steered me to, I might have very well been one of the soldiers at Normandy on D-Day, who knows. Life is so curious that way.

Back to the job offer Al was suggesting I consider, there was plenty of danger. Just getting to Pearl Harbor was full of risk because of Japanese submarines. Plus, many feared another attack on Pearl Harbor. An inducement was a 25% pay increase to attract workers, as in yours truly.

If I accepted the offer, the boat trip to Hawaii, instead of taking 5 days, would be 10 days because of having to zig-zag the Pacific Ocean to dodge Japanese subs and their treacherous torpedoes. But first I'd have to travel cross country by train to San Francisco before boarding an old, WW1 cargo ship to go to Honolulu.

It was a huge decision that, when I weighed all the factors, including the stigma of not being in the service, I decided to apply for the job. Another chapter in my life was about to begin.

CHAPTER 18

ALL ABOARD, BUT WAIT, DON'T LEAVE WITHOUT ME! (1943)

Before I describe the train trip to San Francisco, I briefly want to go back in time to my pre-teen years. My friends and I had an mustachioed Italian barber named Marco, who would give us our haircuts that cost fifty cents.

Marco was an excellent barber but he had a volatile temper that he dealt with in an unusual and funny way. Whenever Marco was about to curse up a storm, which you'd expect would have been in Italian, instead, he would yell out, "Sacramento, California!" (Don't ask me why he picked that but we definitely found it hysterical, among ourselves that is, and it very heavily figures into this vignette.)

I heard Marco yell "Sacramento, California!" so many times and silently laughed to myself each time. So, when it came time to board the train at Penn Station in 1943 to leave for San Francisco and then board a WW1 cargo vessel to go to Pearl Harbor, you'll see why I mention Marco.

We were to cross the U.S. on a 3 ½ day and night train trip. I had an upper berth on a Pullman train, which included meals in the dining car, all of which was quite an adventure for me. At 21, I had never even left New York City. So seeing the country go by out my window was pretty fascinating.

Toward the very end of the trip, I distinctly remember the conductor calling out "Next stop, Sacramento, California," and stating that we would be in the station for about twenty minutes. Sacramento?? Here was my opportunity to actually see the Sacramento that I had heard Marco yell about so many times and maybe get a clue to why he shouted it instead of swearing.

I got off the train and went out into the street. I was stunned by the clean streets, lots of flowers and the beautiful trees lining the avenue. I thought to myself, "Compared to New York City, this is heaven." To say the least, I was very impressed with California's state capital. So much so that I walked around mesmerized by the beauty of that city, until suddenly, I remembered the conductor had said, "Twenty minutes." Holy mackerel! I'd better get back on that train before it leaves without me! All my luggage and travel orders were in my berth!

I literally ran back to the station just in time to see a slowly moving train pulling out. I ran as fast as my feet could take me and, luckily, was just able to grab the handle and pull myself up onto the train. Oh my God, that was too close for comfort. As I entered the car I took a deep sigh, like I had just avoided a colossal nightmare. Relieved doesn't begin to describe how I felt.

But, as I walked through the cars, a deeply disturbing feeling came over me. Keep in mind, after traveling for three and a half days and being the outgoing and chatty person, I am, I had talked to almost everybody on the train. Now, as I looked around, I thought it really strange that suddenly nobody looked familiar!

I hurriedly went from car to car but I didn't recognize a soul. Panic was starting to set in. Finally, it dawned on me and confirmed my worst fear... I was on the wrong train! (If OMG had been in the parlance in those days, I might have shouted "OMG!" Or maybe I should have shouted "Sacramento, California!" like Marco?)

Frantic, I found the conductor and, almost breathlessly explained what I had done, that all my papers for the job in Pearl Harbor, my wallet, my luggage, everything was on another train going I had no idea where. He began to laugh but, frankly, I failed to see the humor.

"Relax kid, you're one lucky guy" the conductor said. "What do you mean?" I replied because I certainly didn't feel lucky. "Well, this train is heading west. Your train is still in the station." "So what do I do? I asked?

The conductor continued, "We will stop at Martinez, California, in about ten minutes. You get off there and pretty soon your train will be coming down the same tracks after we pull out. When it stops briefly, you hop on and you'll be back on your original train." I felt so relieved I thought I might pass out.

Sure enough, the conductor was right. I got back on my train only I was so nervous I had to use the bathroom. Afterwards, I splashed some cold water in my face like I had just awakened from a bad dream. I was so nervous and in such a hurry I didn't even dry it all off.

As I walked into the first car I thought to myself, "Please God, let me recognize somebody, anybody, so I know I'm on the right train!" Finally I saw Gladys, a middle-aged woman from Yonkers.

I rushed up to her, "Gladys, it's you!" I said as I gave her a big hug that left her a bit taken aback. "Of course it's me," she said in puzzlement. "Why are you perspiring?"

"Oh, I washed my face, I guess I didn't dry off." Now she was concerned. "You look like you've seen a ghost. Are you okay, Jerry?" "Oh, sure, Gladys, fit as a fiddle."

But Gladys wasn't convinced. "Where have you been all this time?" "Oh, that, uh, well, I've been in the bathroom." "All this time?" "Yeah, well I guess something from lunch didn't agree with me." "But we haven't had lunch yet," she replied. "Oh, I meant breakfast." Gladys was still rather worried about me. "Why don't you sit down and relax, Jerry." "Great idea, Gladys as soon as I check a few things."

I rushed over to my seat and everything was in perfect order. I ran into other people who also were curious as to where I had been. I gave them each a version of the "Lunch didn't agree with me," only I was careful to say "breakfast." I'm not sure anyone believed me but it beat saying, "I'm such a dumb ass, I jumped on the wrong train."

I can laugh about it now but I can assure you I didn't find it too funny then. And, to this day, I still don't know why Marco would shout, "Sacramento, California." Apparently, I'm just going to have to live with never knowing. Oh well.

CHAPTER 19

DESTINATION HONOLULU, UNLESS WE GET TORPEDOED (1943)

I'll say this about myself, once I make a decision I try to see it through. I got that from my parents and I'm eternally grateful for it. That said, the boat trip from San Francisco to Honolulu gave me great doubts if I had, in fact, made the right decision, although it was far too late to back out now. Put it this way, the trip across the Pacific on that dilapidated boat was not exactly the Queen Mary luxury cruise, plus we could be blown up by a Japanese torpedo at any minute.

Trust me, I'm not generally a complainer or an alarmist, quite the opposite. But this trip severely tested my basic good nature. And it made the thousand or so fellow passengers, soldiers, marines and civilians like myself (on our way to work at the Navy Yard) very crabby and frightened to say the least. And I'll explain why.

First the ship, the U.S.S. Tyler was an old WW1 cargo ship, which had seen better days. At least I hope it had. And, the food, to say it was basically inedible doesn't do it justice, or injustice in this case. Everything was powder: eggs, milk, potatoes and soup. Yuck. Suffice it to say, the kitchen was referred to as the "Slop Chest." Put it this way, as we ate, we didn't exactly wish each other "bon appétit."

Also, there were no showers on board. That meant, after a day or so, being below deck in the sleeping area was intolerable because the smell was overwhelming. Everyone wound up sleeping on the deck. And there was the small item that we were in constant danger of being attacked by a Japanese sub. We kept zig-jagging for 10 days until finally...there was Honolulu harbor. And none too soon for my liking.

Imagine our delight to be greeted by beautiful Hawaiian girls doing the hula. We were ecstatic to leave the ship, have our feet on the ground and get to take a shower asap! (Not to mention eat food that wasn't made of powder.)

When I arrived in Honolulu, the only person I knew was my childhood friend, Al Glassman, who was the sole reason I had taken the job. He had arranged so that I would room with him and another Brighton Beach kid, Avey Benfield, whom Al had been buddies with. Al and Avey had arrived about three months before I did so, by then, they knew their way around Honolulu.

Just being in Pearl Harbor was a shock to me, being 21 and having never left New York City. In the harbor were battleships, destroyers, aircraft carriers waiting to be deployed. Next to our housing was Hickam Field where sat row after sat row after row of B-17 bombers. Generally they would take off very early in the morning and hopefully return. My room was so close, when they took off it felt like the roof was coming off. If I looked out my window I could actually see the pilot's face.

Though we were 1,000 miles from the front lines, war was in the air. We had a 10 P.M. blackout curfew with the lights off or the shades drawn so the Japanese could not see us as targets. Though I got used to it over time, the stress was so great that only at work, where I ground cylinders to go into our fighter planes, could I relax to some degree.

Almost the entire world was at war and democracy was at stake against the brutal fascism of Hitler, Mussolini and Tojo. Leading our country was FDR, a man whose disability kept him in a wheelchair much of the time, while in London, the British were led by Winston Churchill a man, by today's standards, I believe would have been labeled an alcoholic.

It was a testament to the remarkable courage, sacrifice and strength of both men and those of the allied forces to somehow save the world. (All these years later it sometimes amazes me to think about.)

Anyway, that first evening in Honolulu, Al and Avey took me to the Moana Hotel. With a gentle warm breeze in the air, I sat in the courtyard with a cocktail facing the Pacific Ocean and being serenaded by Ray Kinney and his Royal Hawaiians. And once again, there were more hula dancers, whom, I confess, I never seemed to tire of.

As for my work, I was assigned as a "Machinist Apprentice" (meaning the lowest rung on the ladder) to the Ford Island Naval Air Station. Al was a Machinist 2nd Class and Avey was a welder at the Navy Yard. We three lived together in Naval Civilian Housing which was only 10 minutes from the Navy Yard, so for Al and Avey, getting to work was a short, safe, bus trip. But, for me, I had to take a motorboat launch that could transport 40 people and took a tedious (and always potentially dangerous) 20 minutes.

Avey had a Philippine girlfriend named Phoebe with whom he had a hot and heavy romance. Unfortunately, Avey let it interfere with work and called in sick way too often. Al and I tried to explain to him what he already should have known.

U.S. soldiers were dying all over the world so we were damn fortunate to have these jobs. Yes, we were always in some danger just being in Pearl Harbor as the threat of the Japanese re-attacking was ever present but we were 1000% luckier than the poor guys on the front lines.

Avey had to know we were right. But, being a happy-go-lucky ladies man, he joked, "All's fair in love and war, guys." Sadly, that would turn out to be the cause of his ultimate demise as you will soon see.

CHAPTER 20

CANDID CAMERA, HAWAIIAN STYLE (1944)

Another one of the friends I made while at Pearl Harbor was Leon Garden, a Jewish young man from St. Louis. On Sunday, our day off, we were walking in downtown Honolulu and we noticed a sidewalk photographer taking photos of the soldiers, sailors and marines as they passed in front of his camera. As he took their photo, he would hand them a card.

The card notified the subject that his picture had just been snapped candidly and that the photographer's company would sell him four postcard-sized photos for one dollar. It was actually a great deal because the service man only needed to put the address of his friend or relative add a stamp, and bingo he had an instant postcard of himself overseas, so to speak.

If you were interested, the photographer's partner would sign you up and take your money. Three days later your pictures would be ready in a shop about three blocks away. If you weren't satisfied with the results, they would either refund the money or take the pictures over again.

Lee and I stood and watched for about fifteen minutes but the photographer, apparently not much of a salesman, hardly spoke. As a result, the streets were littered with these cards. Evidently, the serviceman had not been convinced enough that his photo had really been taken.

We picked up a card from the sidewalk and walked over to the shop where the pick-ups were made. We had decided to apply for a job working part-time. We decided Leon would collect the money and I would be the photographer, even though I had never owned a camera in my life.

We arrived at the shop easily enough. It was a greeting card store that also sold stationary. What a great idea, I thought. While people are picking up the pictures, they could buy a greeting card. I asked a woman if I could speak to the owner and was informed she was the owner. I explained I would like to snap pictures like the fellow we saw. "Have you any experience?" she asked. I confessed, "None, but I'm great at following instructions."

She was impressed with my "can do attitude." "That's all right," she said, "I could teach you. It's lucky you came by today because I have to replace the man you saw. He's going back home on leave shortly and I need a replacement." I piped up, "Well, I'm your man."

Right there on the street, she showed me how to use the camera. She explained the camera was a Devry movie camera rigged up to take single shots and the important thing was to center the subject in the view finder and not cut off any heads. (Imagine a job where you're told "don't cut off any heads.") Also, she pointed out that if three servicemen are walking together, emphasize that all three are in the picture.

We took the camera home where I practiced on Lee. We saw very good possibilities with this new venture. Each man would get 10% of the gross. It was almost always sunny but the sun had to be over my shoulder. We could work three or four hours a day and a little longer on a Sunday, our day off from our regular jobs.

Lee and I took over that corner. I talked it up real good and in no time at all I was selling one of every two pictures I snapped. I would average about 400 snaps a day and sell 200. That's $200 and 10% was $20 for me and $20 for Lee. Multiply $20 by 6. That equals $120, plus Sunday we would work five hours and make $25 a day for each of us. We were making more money from this part-time job than on our regular jobs!

There was one rather scary glitch, however. One day we were working and I noticed a civilian surreptitiously checking us out and even following us. It was eerie. Finally, he came over and flashed Navy intelligence credentials. Yikes! It went from eerie to scary, real quick.

I instantly realized this was serious business. He started to interrogate me like I was a spy and I got pretty nervous. His main line of interrogation was what information did I get from each serviceman who paid the $1. I told him, their address i.e. if they were on a ship etc. "That part is over starting right now. Do I make myself clear, young man?!" I gulped. "Totally. Completely. Got it." I said trying to keep from stammering.

He went on to explain that any info like that was potentially dangerous. He basically said, "Loose lips, sink ships." So from that moment on, all we got from the serviceman was his $1 and where he could pick up the postcards. If he didn't show up, that was his business, but where he was stationed was none of our business. I was very relieved not to have gotten in trouble.

My schedule was working at Ford Island 4:00 P.M. until midnight. I'd go home, get some sleep, and start taking pictures about 9:00 A.M. after a good breakfast at Hollister's Drugstore. (I loved their toasted bear claws with butter on it.)

The irony was that I was sending so much money home to Mom, she came to the conclusion I must have taken up gambling, something I had never done in my life. I finally convinced her everything was kosher but it wasn't easy. She just couldn't get over all the money seemingly pouring in. As always, I was delighted to make her life easier.

CHAPTER 21

RACISM WAS ALIVE AND NOT SWELL
(1943)

When I arrived in Pearl Harbor, Hawaii, I was assigned to work at the Ford Island Naval Air Station where I was a machinist's helper. There were about eighteen men in the machine shop. As I became acquainted, I realized that I was the only Jew and a man who would become my good friend, Urban Richards, was the only African-American.

I worked the 4:00 P.M. to midnight shift with about 12 men who were from the South. In 1943, the Ku Klux Klan was still a powerful force in the south. And even in parts of the north, there was lots of racism against African-Americans and Jews. (Unfortunately, the Klan is back on the rise now and anti-semitism is growing rapidly in Europe. It's as though we humans never seem to learn.)

Growing up in Brooklyn, with Jews, Italians, Irish and African-Americans, we all got along. I don't ever remember any discrimination. In the apartment house, next to the one we lived in, the janitor was African-American and he lived there with his two sons, Leroy and Julian. The brothers went on to become star athletes in high school.

Billy Ratigan, an Irish kid, taught me how to ride a bicycle he had received as a Christmas gift. I played baseball with Italians, Jews, Irish, and anyone who could catch and hit. Surprisingly as it may sound, I never encountered any prejudice until I came to Pearl Harbor. I was in for a rude shock.

The unique thing was that Honolulu was a very cosmopolitan city that had lots of inter-racial marriages—Chinese and Hawaiians, Portuguese and Middle Easterners,

Japanese, African-Americans and Filipinos. But in the shop I worked in, the Southerners dominated and also brought their prejudices with them.

Around 7:00 P.M., we would break for dinner. There was a cafeteria near the shop where Urban and I would eat together. I found him to be a very intelligent gentleman. He was seventeen years older than I was and had grown up in Chicago. I felt I could learn a lot from being in his company. He had been around more than I had and was a University of Chicago graduate.

One day, one of the Southerner good old boys came over to me. "Rosie," he said, "the guys don't much like the way you cozy up to the nig*er, eating with him and hanging out with him during the breaks."

At that stage in my life, actually any stage in my life, I didn't like being bullied. I told this Georgia cracker that I was from New York and in New York we don't discriminate just because someone is of a different color. "Go back and tell your boys that I'll eat and be friendly with whoever I want to and if anyone objects, let them tell me to my face and I'll handle it from there." (Pretty tough talk for a guy 5'6" but I could back it up if someone got me mad enough.)

Urban got wind of what was going on and, given his life experience, he cautioned me to be very careful—that these guys could be dangerous. "Maybe," he said, "we should do as they say." My attitude was nothing doing. "If we do that," I replied, "then they win and I don't want to back down." Well, evidently, whatever I told the KKKer registered because, thankfully, I never heard another word from any of them after that incident.

However, one thing happened in the shop and it was most likely an accident instead of on purpose. One night, I was working on a lathe while next to my machine was a drill press. One of the "good ole boys" from Mississippi had to drill a hole in a four-inch block of aluminum. The proper way to do it would be to clamp the aluminum block to the base of the machine and set the drill press on high speed.

The reason for high speed is because aluminum is a soft metal and the drill won't do the job unless it's on high speed. Well, that day this clown came to work drunk, though I don't know how the foreman of the shop missed it. Instead of clamping the block to the machine, he held it in his hand and then lowered the drill bit. As soon as the drill touched the block of aluminum, it flew out of his hand and struck me in my right eye.

The force of the metal knocked me completely off my feet. As I struggled to get back up, I put my right hand to my eye and it was full of blood. I was rushed to the emergency hospital on the island. The attending doctor told me I was a very lucky guy. "Another quarter of an inch and you would have lost your right eye." (I couldn't help but think of that imaginary angel on my shoulder, which at times like that, didn't seem so imaginary.)

He shaved off my right eyebrow and put in stitches to close the wound. He did a very skillful job because it left no visible scars. He said I should go home and rest. I was a very patriotic guy and I remember telling him that men are dying out there on the islands in the Pacific and I was not about to go home as long as I could see out of the other eye.

With one eye covered with a bandage, I returned to the shop. Zapatocky, the foreman, put his arm around me and asked me quietly if I was going to sue. "No," I replied. "It was an accident." I could see him breathe a sigh of relief.

Then the guy who caused the accident came over to me, put his arm around me and said, "Rosie, you're a white Jew." That was his way of complimenting me on how I handled the incident. From that day forward up to the day I went home, I never had any more trouble from the southerners. We definitely weren't friends but they respected me and no longer tried to tell me who to hang out with. I felt it was progress and left it at that.

There was another incident of horrible racism that I remember to this day. I was in Honolulu one night with Avey and Al and we saw a terrible fist fight. Some drunken sailors were beating the hell out of some Japanese-American soldiers. Keep in mind, these soldiers were our guys, fighting and dying in Europe. But to the drunk sailors they were just "Japs."

The three of us were going to break it up but there were more than a half dozen other sailors forming a ring to stop any do-gooders from interfering. I'll never forget it, American sailors brutally beating American soldiers just because they had Japanese ancestry. It sickened me. As Mark Twain said, "The more I learn about man, the more I like my dog."

As for my job, Machinist 3rd class, my work was hard and tedious. Every day I would get big cylinders, approximately 18" high and 12" across that would ultimately go into the engines of our fighter planes. What I had to do, eight hours a day, 5 days a week, was, with the aid of an external radial drill press, "bore out" the insides of the cylinders to a 1/1000th of an inch tolerance.

As tough as the work and working conditions were, I never for a moment forgot about our guys on the front lines. And, at the end of the long hot day, exhausted as I would be, I always finished 3 cylinders. To me that meant 3 more U.S. fighter planes would be able to fight our enemies. And it felt good to know I had helped.

CHAPTER 22

WE THOUGHT FOR SURE WE WERE GONERS (1944)

In 1943, when I told people I'd be leaving for Pearl Harbor to be a machinist in the war effort, they thought I made a bad move. "The Japanese are coming back to finish the job," I was told. And I said, "I'll take my chances." But there was one unusually cloudy Pearl Harbor afternoon in 1944 when I wasn't so sure about "my chances."

As usual, I was in the launch taking me to Ford Island for my 4 p.m. to midnight shift, when suddenly the sky was filled with planes. They seemed to come out of nowhere. But here they were—diving and pulling out of the dives at the last minute. Because of the clouds, you couldn't see them but we could certainly hear the almost deafening roar that was truly frightening. Frankly, we all thought we were dead ducks.

And yet, for some reason, I was surprisingly calm. There was certainly no place to hide.

And yet, I thought to myself, it's in God's hands now as to whether I live or die.

Just then, a plane went into a steep dive over the Navy Yard itself and, shockingly, never came out of the dive. But it wasn't a Japanese plane, it was one of ours! It crashed in the Navy Yard hitting a bus that was transporting workers to the various shops. All this happened about a hundred yards from where I was in the launch.

When the plane hit the bus, we saw a big ball of flames shoot up to the sky. Suddenly it was over. The "raid" over Pearl Harbor had been a "mock attack" to improve ground air defense alert. Everyone in our launch suddenly breathed sighs of relief. (A month later in the newspaper it was disclosed that 27 people died in this tragic accident.)

As my heart slowly stopped racing, I had a flashback of a similar scare only two weeks earlier. I was at a shoe shine stand in the Navy housing getting my shoes shined when suddenly the ground shook and the chair I was sitting on lurched. The Honolulu Star Bulletin reported that a barge loaded with ammunition had exploded and several sailors lost their lives.

Only weeks before that, I was riding on a bus going along Dillingham Boulevard toward Pearl Harbor Navy Yard. We were riding alongside an airfield for Marine pilots. Suddenly, I saw a Marine with a flag in each hand frantically waving to attract the attention of a pilot coming in for a landing to let him know he had forgotten to lower his wheels.

Sure enough, the plane landed on its belly and burst into flames. The pilot jumped out and rolled on the ground but, remarkably, he was not badly hurt. In fact, he was immediately put into another plane and told to take off. Later, I was told that they did this to make sure pilots didn't lose their nerve.

The bottom line for me, given all I experienced and saw, no matter where you are in a war, it's damn scary.

CHAPTER 23

DADDY NEEDS A NEW PAIR OF SHOES (1945)

At my Defense Plant job, I worked diligently, did whatever was asked of me and basically just kept my nose to the grindstone. (Pun intended.) On my time off from work I stayed out of card games and crap games and the gambling that was going on in the naval civilian housing even though it was 100% legal. That's right, the Navy set up a casino featuring crap tables, roulette tables, blackjack, and slot machines. (Vegas, Navy style?)

You see the Navy knew that if you gather a bunch of civilians together from all over the U.S. there would be crooked card and crap games and that would lead to knifings and killings when the cheating was discovered. By the way, to get into the gambling casino run by the Navy all you had to do was show a paid-up rent receipt. Another interesting thing, our mail was censored, so you couldn't write home about it.

Meanwhile, the contract I signed with the Navy Department was for eighteen months. I had stayed twenty-two months and decided it was time to go home on leave. I remember boarding the Lurline, a cruise ship that had been converted to a troopship. I was given a bunk to sleep in, a double decker and I slept on the top bunk.

Aboard the ship, there were soldiers, sailors, marines and civilians all going home on leave. The war was still going full blast. Although we were getting the upper hand in Europe after the Battle of the Bulge, in the Pacific it was still very rough. Kamikaze pilots from the Japanese air force were diving into our ships and doing lots of damage, causing many deaths among our Navy personnel and sinking lots of our ships.

The first day out to sea on my trip home on leave, someone started a crap game right next to my bunk. I tried my best to resist getting into the game. I had five hundred dollars with me and I intended to still have it when it was time to disembark the ship. Then I thought I should just take fifty dollars and play with that, win or lose, just to get it out of my system. So that is what I did. I stood there watching the game and then it was my turn to roll the dice.

I figured I'd start out small and test my luck. I rolled the dice and bet two dollars. Well, I won! So now I doubled the bet and I won again! I repeated that two more times and had made four passes in a row.

Just then, with lots of money in the pot, a burly and rough merchant marine who looked like Victor McLaughlin (a popular actor), put his size thirteen shoe on the money. "Let me see those dice." Nobody was going to argue with the likes of him. He picked up the dice, slowly held them up to the light and rolled them around with his fingers. I got very nervous because they weren't my dice and I didn't know if they were crooked or not. And I had a bad feeling if they were crooked old Victor, who might have been twice my size, was going to break up some things, starting with me.

Finally, someone shouted, "Come on. Give the kid back the dice. He's cooling off." Finally, Vic was convinced the dice were on the up and up. Whew.

To make a long story short, I made eleven passes in a row. I remember stuffing money in my pants pockets when it was over. I was so nervous my right leg began to quiver and I couldn't stop it. Finally, at the end, with my pants pockets bulging with money, I went into the bathroom in order to straighten out the bills and count how much money I had won. It came to eight hundred and sixty-five dollars!

Just then, an African-American came into the bathroom and said to me, "Man, you got a 'golden arm.' You and me, we're gonna clean up in L.A." I replied, "Sorry, but I'm headed for New York." I felt bad because he was so disappointed. I can still see the look on his face.

The next day the crap game was on again. I thought maybe lady luck would be with me again. This time, I decided to risk two hundred and blew it in about twenty minutes. I learned my lesson. As fast as I had won the money, thankfully only $200 of it, I lost it even faster.

CHAPTER 24

WHOEVER SAID "WAR IS HELL…" (1944-1945)

Well into my first year working at my defense job in Hawaii, I suddenly received a 1A card from my draft board. This was very serious business because it meant I could very easily lose my job and get drafted. I immediately showed it to my shop foreman Mr. Zapatocky whom we called Zap. I was told not to concern myself because there were about a dozen of us who had received 1A cards on Ford Island.

We were all going to submit to a physical at Schofield Barracks Army Camp just outside of Honolulu and, if we passed the physical, we would be sworn into the Navy and put on inactive duty. We would go back to work, as usual, not have to wear a uniform and we would collect our paychecks just as before. (But not having actually served on active duty, we were not entitled to any benefits.)

I mention all of this because our friend and roommate, Avey, wasn't so lucky. Maybe lucky isn't the right word because Avey knew with his record of excessively taking days off to be with his girlfriend, he was playing with fire. So it was Avey was ordered to report to his draft board for induction into the service.

Avey was a great guy but we couldn't have been more different. I may have grown up to be a very serious kid, maybe even overly serious because I lost my father so early, whereas Avey, having had such a solid background, was a party animal. You couldn't help but like him but at the same time, we wished he would have taken his job and situation more seriously. Al and I worried about Avey and, sure enough, it caught up with him.

About a year later, late 1944, as a part-time sidewalk photographer, imagine my surprise when I looked into the viewfinder and there stood Avey Benfield in full

Army uniform! He was a paratrooper. He was in Honolulu temporarily before he would be shipped out to one of the islands in the Pacific. Well, as it turned out he was sent to Okinawa and, sadly, was killed there. You can imagine how devastated we were when we got the news. At 23, Avey's life was over.

So it was when I got that leave I just described I returned to New York for 30 days. I remember thinking that the right thing to do would be to visit Avey's parents as they lived close by and I was the last person to talk to Avey before he was killed. I had never met Avey's parents before and, to be honest, I walked around the block 6 times before I got the nerve to knock on the door. As it turned out, it was one of the worst days of my life.

Avey's parents naturally wanted to know why Avey was sent back to be inducted and not me or Al? His mother broke down crying as her husband comforted her. It's said honesty is the best policy, but how could I tell them the truth that Avey had not taken the job seriously enough? I just couldn't. So I blamed it on Navy bureaucracy.

As I left their house, I, too, broke down in tears. Whoever was the first to say, "War is hell," knew what they were talking about.

CHAPTER 25

PEACE AT LAST, THANK GOD! (1945)

During the fall of 1945, I remember standing on the corner of Kings Highway and 16th Street across from Dubrow's Cafeteria with my friend Mike Dolansky and Harvey Lembeck. All three of us had been overseas and shared a lot of our experiences and readjusting to life after the war as were millions of men and women. Among the subjects we chatted about over a beer was our plans for the future.

Many guys coming back from war tried to transfer skills they used in the military to civilian life, though obviously arm to arm combat wouldn't come in handy, until maybe now with UFC fights on ESPN. (And no, I don't watch them.)

We were all about the same age. I remember Harvey telling us he intended to enroll in The American Academy of Dramatic Arts under the GI Bill. We wished him luck and boy, did he find it as he had a great career.

As for me, going back to school wasn't really an option, for two reasons. One, I was never a great student. Even with working 30 hours a week, I graduated high school but I didn't get the best grades. And two, despite my years during WW2 working at the Ford Island Naval Air Station in Pearl Harbor, I wasn't eligible for the G.I. Bill. Most importantly, I needed to make money to continue to support my mother and brother, although Artie was starting to do real well for himself.

One thing, I didn't want to use were my machinist skills because I discovered that, unfortunately, many guys in that profession were anti-Semitic. With the name Rosenblum, combined with the fact that when I get bullied, I don't back down, I could see a future of me as a machinist with a black eye saying, "Yeah, but you should see the other guy.

The second reason is I was tired of working and getting dirty and greasy and needing to take frequent showers to wash off work grime. I wanted a job where I would wear a suit and feel like a mensch. I guess I wanted to be a professional mensch.

I stayed in touch with Harvey who, as I mentioned earlier, followed through on his plan to become an actor. After he graduated, he auditioned for the part of a sailor from Brooklyn in the hit Broadway show Mr. Roberts starring Henry Fonda. He got the part and was terrific. A talent scout brought him out to Hollywood after the play had its run.

He then went on to appear in many movies. One of the best was Stalag 17 starring William Holden. He also had a reoccurring part in one of my favorite TV comedy series of all time, "Bilko" or later, "The Phil Silvers Show." (Ran from 1955 to 1959.)

If you love to laugh, Google "YouTube Bilko Orders Hairpins and Bubblegum." Harvey has a great part in that episode. (I know, it's kinda funny a 98 year old man is telling you to use the Google machine.)

Many years after that street corner meeting, I ran into Harvey on West 45th Street in the Theater District. He told me that he was starring in a show just a few feet from where we were standing. It was called Wedding Breakfast. Also starring in it were Lee Grant and Lee Phillips.

Later on, Harvey opened an acting school for budding comedians. His son, Michael Lembeck, also became an actor and now directs TV shows. In fact, Michael directed a young actress friend of mine, Abigail Breslin, well known for her Academy Award nominated performance in the hit movie "Little Miss Sunshine." (My chapter about Abbie is the second to last in this book so pay attention because there might be a surprise quiz.)

Sadly, in 1982, and far too soon, Harvey passed away from a heart attack at age fifty-eight. He was one terrific guy. Shortly before he died, I ran into him quite unexpectedly at the Israel Levin Center, a senior center in Venice, California. He was a member of a lodge called the Eddie Cantor Lodge. They were mostly guys who had been in show business and were retired. They had heard about the Levin Center from a documentary called Number Our Days, which won an Academy Award.

A professor of anthropology and gerontology at USC, Barbara Meyerhof, produced the film. As a result of that film, the Eddie Cantor Lodge Members decided to provide coffee and bagels every Sunday for the seniors. They became benefactors and did lots of good work. They also earned my utmost admiration.

After the war, Harvey had found his path and made it an incredible success. For many of us, post-war, the journey was a little more difficult to find. (That said, of course, anything beat being at war.)

CHAPTER 26

WILL THE REAL PUSSY ROSENHEIM STAND UP? (1945)

In the winter of 1945 it was extremely cold in New York. I may have felt it more because of having been in Hawaii for almost two years. I was in between jobs, none of which seemed to have a future. But I wasn't the only guy struggling to find a career after the war. Some of my friends, who had been mustered out of the service, were standing on the corner freezing, too. We were all receptive when someone suggested we go to Florida and get jobs just for the winter.

My mother was fine with the idea because she knew after my years during the war, I needed some kind of break. So, with her blessing, I was off to the sunshine state.

Ellie Bishop, had a 1939 Chevy that the four of us piled into: me, Ellie, Sid Bernstein and Lee Camer. The trip took three days but the most amazing part is Ellie's Chevy didn't break down. Thankfully.

Once in Florida, we split up and went to various hotels seeking work. I walked into the Atlantis Hotel on Collins Avenue and saw a guy about 50 years old talking in such a loud voice you could hear him all over the lobby. He was a little guy with one shirttail sticking out of the front of his pants. To me he looked like a bookmaker. (Which is exactly what he was.)

Pussy Rosenheim (how's that for a name?) was not only a bookmaker, he was also a partner in the hotel. His other two partners were Otto Halbreich, a dress manufacturer and Ben Novak who grew up in the hotel business. (Of the three, Novak was the only one who knew how to run a hotel.)

Mr. Rosenheim hired me as a bellhop, right on the spot. (I always called him Mr. Rosenheim because I wasn't going to ever call him Pussy or Mr. Pussy.) The next day when I showed up they gave me a uniform and explained my duties, which included helping guests with their luggage, delivering buckets of ice to guest rooms, emptying ashtrays in the card room, running the elevator and, in general, trying to make myself useful.

The Atlantis was considered to be an upscale hotel. One of the guests was Sol Rutchick, a horse trainer at tracks like Hialeah. Another guest was William P. Goldman, the owner of GGG Clothes one of the very best brands in upscale men's clothing stores all over the U.S.

We found a place to live in South Beach, the Catskill Hotel. (An odd name in Florida, huh?) It was located right next to a dog track. At night when I was exhausted and desperately needed sleep, all I would hear was, "And there goes Rusty!" Rusty was the mechanical rabbit that the greyhounds chased around the track.

One Saturday night after I was working at the Atlantis for a few weeks, I noticed an attractive young lady sitting all alone in the lobby. I was due to get off about 9 P.M. and, after we became acquainted, I asked Bernice out. She accepted so I took her to the Colonial Inn.

The Colonial was a fancy casino in Miami Beach where gambling was legal. One thing you couldn't help but notice is that the women who were gambling at the crap tables and roulette wheels were wearing expensive evening dresses and were dripping with jewelry. (Rumor was there were highly skilled pickpockets working the place.)

Sure enough, every two minutes the women would touch their ears to see if their earrings were still on, or nonchalantly check their wrists to see if their diamond bracelets were still there, or casually touch their neck to see if their diamond-studded necklace was still there. (Apparently, being rich is not that easy.)

As it got late, we left by cab back to the Atlantis. But Bernice told the cab driver to stop a block before the hotel and she would proceed the rest of the way on foot. The next day, I found out that Bernice was the niece of one of the hotel owners, Otto Halbreich. I guess she didn't care to be seen with a lowly bellhop on a Saturday night. (That said we stayed friends and she gave me a sexy photo of her I still have to this day. Go figure.)

After a few months, you could say opportunity came knocking. One of the "important" guests was one of the owners of Leighton's, an upscale men's Manhattan clothing store. William Schlesinger was impressed with my work habits and said when I got back to New York I should look him up because he would have a job for me.

And that's what I did. At Leighton's I had visions of becoming a retail clothing salesman. Instead, I was in the basement stockroom ticketing men's furnishings and unpacking shipments—in other words, a stock clerk. In other words, pretty boring.

I worked there several months and saw no future in it. But just getting a taste of the men's clothing business led me to Kallen's Clothing Store where I had twice been a customer. Through sheer persistence and laying on the charm, I got an entry-level sales job at Kallen's and began working there in March 1947.

You could say, even during WWII I was a kid. At Kallen's, I became a man. I had finally found my life's work. Or had it found me? (Meanwhile, I would occasionally have nightmares and hear a loudspeaker, "And there goes Rusty!")

CHAPTER 27

THE POLICE AND I CRACKED THE CASE (1947)

I still remember my very first day on the job at Kallen's Clothes, and the beginning of what would be a 50-year career in the men's clothing business. The two-story building was over two hundred years old. It was so old it had a weather vane on the roof. (I always loved that.)

We were situated on two floors. The first floor stocked slacks and topcoats. I was instructed to stay downstairs and greet the customers. If the customer wanted to look at suits, I was to tell him to walk up one flight to the second floor. Okay, so now you have the layout.

I vividly remember my very first day on the job because it was thrilling in a way I could never have anticipated. We opened at 9 A.M. and at about 9:30, the door bursts open, a man races right over to the pant rack and then immediately runs out the door back onto the street. What the hell?

I thought the whole thing was very strange, indeed. About twenty seconds after he left, two more men burst into the store. One of them asks me what the man who exited so hurriedly did while he was there. I told him he went over to the pant rack. The two men quickly went to the rack and shook it. We all heard a "plink" and when we looked under the rack, there, lying on the floor, was the biggest diamond ring I had ever seen. They scooped up the ring and ran out the door. I felt like I was in a Buster Keaton movie. (If you're too young to recognize the name, go to YouTube and type Buster Keaton because he was a comedy genius.)

So what actually happened in our store? I found out that evening, after reading a newspaper on the way home. You see, the guy who planted the ring in the pant rack had been looking at diamond rings in an upscale jewelry shop at 6th Avenue. Suddenly, he scooped up a handful of rings and ran out.

A description of the thief was given and the direction he was running. The two guys, who shook the rack, were detectives hot on the thief's trail and finally they caught him. Anyway, that's how my first day started. That was March 1947.

As immodest as it sounds, I went on to have a long and successful salesman career. But frankly, there was never more excitement than the first hour of the first day when I "helped" crack a diamond jewelry theft case. Okay, I just basically pointed the cops in the right direction. But, after the arrest, they came back and did, in fact, say I was a "huge help." (I tried to sell them some clothes but they didn't seem interested. Oh well, nothing ventured, nothing gained.)

CHAPTER 28

THE ICEBOX CHRISTMAS (1947)

The following is a Christmas story but it's not like one that could be turned into a movie starring Jimmy Stewart. Groucho Marx would be more like it, or, to be more contemporary, I could see Will Ferell playing me.

It was December 26, 1947 and it snowed hard from morning to night without a let-up. Even though it was the day after Christmas, I didn't dare take the day off from working at Kallen's Clothes. I was 26 still trying like crazy to impress my boss and solidify my position as a valued salesman. The point being, so focused on work, I paid little attention to the weather outside.

"Baby it's cold outside," NYC blizzard, 1947.

We used to close the store at 6 P.M. and then I would walk a few blocks to the subway. On this particular evening, I was kind of shocked about how much snow had piled up but I didn't realize it would be a record blizzard. As it happens, I was bringing home a bottle of Canadian Club whiskey given to me as a one-day belated Christmas present from one of the clothing manufacturers we dealt with.

I got on the Brighton Express at 34th Street and everything seemed fine until we reached Prospect Park Station. That's when the conductor announced, "This is as far as we go. Everybody off!" Say, what?!

What happened was the tracks were piled so high with snow that the train couldn't go any farther. I asked myself, "How do I get home?" Prospect Park Station was at least ten miles from where I lived.

Grumbling, I walked up a flight of stairs to the street level and saw snow piled higher than I had ever seen it before. There were no cars, no cabs, no buses, just snow everywhere. There wasn't a soul in the street. This was suddenly very serious. One word: Yikes!

Suddenly, I remembered my friend, Sid Lasdon, who had been married only two weeks earlier had rented an apartment just two blocks from where I was standing. Do I dare ring his bell knowing Sid and Shirley, his wife are basically still on their honeymoon? With the snow piled so high who knew when the subway would be back and running. So I walked the two blocks and nervously rang Sid's bell.

When Sid opened the door, on the one hand he was glad to see an old friend from WWII and Ford Island Naval Air Station where we both worked. But the war was long over and he had been lucky enough to meet a wonderful girl and smart enough to marry her.

While Sid was understandably less than thrilled, Shirley made me feel welcome. "Jerry, take off your overcoat and you'll have dinner with us. We have more than enough leftovers from Christmas." Sid also chimed in that the tracks would likely clear in a few hours. So we all dined together and later watched TV. However, they hadn't even yet furnished the 1 bedroom apartment and it was sparse to say the least, but it was warm and cozy, the total opposite of what it was outside.

I opened the bottle of whiskey and toasted the young couple to a long, happy marriage. It was about 11:00 P.M. and I told them that I was going back to Prospect Park Station in the hope that the trains were running again. I remember Shirley telling me if they weren't I should comeback and they'd try to make me comfortable sleeping on the floor. (They didn't yet have a couch or even a large comfortable chair.)

When I got to Prospect Park Station, the trains were still not running. Boy was that a disappointment. Now what was I going to do. Coincidentally, the only other person I saw at the whole station was a mutual friend of Sid's and mine, Leon Camer, who was also stranded. We were delighted to see a friend in the storm.

"Leon," I said. "I just came from Sid's apartment. They offered to let me sleep there tonight. Come with me and they'll have to give you a place to sleep, too." (As I look back, I was sure generous with someone ELSE's accommodations.)

I'll never forget the look on poor Sid's face. Not only had I returned, I had "multiplied," having brought a "guest." Of course, Leon was a friend so what was poor Sid going to do.

Suffice it to say, we finished the bottle that night. The whiskey warmed me and Lee because the blankets were kind of thin. I know, beggars can't be choosers and we were certainly beggars. We actually slept on blankets on the kitchen floor as opposed to the living room because it was further from their bedroom and seemed to give the honeymooners more privacy.

The next morning, we took the Brighton Express back to Manhattan and I went to work, acting like nothing unusual had happened the night before. From then on, I can only hope that every time it snowed really hard in New York, that Sid didn't start worrying and wondering if Jerry was going to show up.

CHAPTER 29

THE TRUE STORY BEHIND TV GUIDE (1948)

Back in 1948, in the very early days of television, I was working for Kallen's Clothes on 7th Avenue near West 38th Street in Manhattan. A very good customer of the store was Charles Ruskin who owned an upscale restaurant in Greenwich Village called Charles' French Restaurant.

One day, Mr. Ruskin came into the store with his son, Lennie. Back then, Army, Navy, Air Force and Marine personnel were being mustered out of the service as the war was over and Lennie one of them. It was time to make a living and start to think about getting married and having a family. Charles Ruskin had a vision of Lennie learning the restaurant business and eventually taking over when his father was ready to retire. However, Lennie had other ideas.

Perhaps a visionary, Lennie had a brainstorm that a person should be able to walk up to a newsstand and buy a guide of some sort that would list all the upcoming shows that were scheduled for television that week. And he followed through with his idea. He took an office in a third-rate office building next to the Old Dixie Hotel on West 42nd Street between 7th and 8th Avenues. I remember selling him a suit and he told me that he was running a one-man business and to "please deliver the suit to my office."

"No problem," I said. "your office is right near the subway entrance I use to get home."

I distinctly remember the delivery and stepping off the elevator. There, on the upper half of the frosted glass office door were the words, "TV Guide." So, you see, folks, that was the very beginning of today's TV Guide.

Lennie's idea caught fire right from the start. Three years later, Walter Annenberg, the billionaire publisher, offered to buy TV Guide for two million dollars. Lennie accepted. He was only twenty-seven and two million dollars 1950 was a fortune. (It ain't bad even now!)

Now, when you read about Walter Annenberg and his accomplishments, he's the one who takes credit for starting TV Guide, but I know better. Oh, by the way, the value of TV Guide on the New York Stock Exchange about four years ago was two billion dollars. That's billion with a B. If Lennie Ruskin is still alive, I wonder how he might feel.

CHAPTER 30

RUN EVERYBODY, THE STORE IS ON FIRE (1949)

I was so determined to be a successful salesman that sometimes it backfired. At age 27, I was new in the business and was working for Kallen's Clothes. Mr. Wolfgang Kallen had promised me a permanent position as a clothing salesman if I showed the "right stuff," so to speak.

I remember on a cold day in January, I was showing a customer some new overcoats that had just arrived. He tried on one of the coats and seemed interested. I spoke about the fabric and workmanship and that the price was very reasonable. Just then, another salesman Dave Rappaport, who had less experience than even I had, tried to get my attention. Dave was related to my boss and had recently emigrated from Belgium. He spoke English but with a pronounced French accent.

"Jerry, I have to talk to you." I whispered, "Not now, Dave. I'm trying to sell a coat." He left but quickly returned. "Jerry, I must talk to you." "Please, Dave, I've almost made a sale here." "But, Jerry. I have to tell you something important." I was starting to get a little impatient with Dave until...

I saw a fireman open the window on the second floor where I was. He was wearing fire-fighting gear, had a hatchet over his shoulder and a fireman's hard-hat on his head. I then realized that all along Dave, in his French accent, had been trying to tell me the store was on fire!

As soon as the customer saw the fireman, he took off the coat and sprinted down the stairs and out the door. Fortunately, the fire, which started in the tailor shop, was fairly small. It was more than embarrassing that I had been so absorbed in trying to make the sale I had been oblivious to what was going on.

The story has a happy ending, however, because not long after, Mr. Kallen kept his word. He signed me to a three-year contract and I joined the retail clothing salesman's union.

That was a big leap forward. It proved that if you work hard, sooner or later your big break will come. (That is, if the store hasn't burned down in the meantime.)

CHAPTER 31

FEELING SORRY FOR MYSELF ALMOST TURNED DEADLY (1949)

In 1949, I was still working at Kallen's Clothes, which I loved but almost all my friends had the weekends off. When you have a weekend off, you can make plans to go places and do things. On very rare occasions I can remember feeling sorry for myself and this is about one of those occasions. I'm not 100% sure, but I think it might have been the last.

One Friday night during summer, a couple friends and I went to an arcade on Ocean Parkway. They had ping pong tables, pinball machines, etc. You could buy an ice cream cone or a bottle of soda. Most importantly, it was a great place to meet girls, etc.

At about 10:00 P.M., one of the guys asked if I would like to go to a great party in Long Beach. They were leaving in a few minutes and I could ride with a guy I knew named Rudy, who had a wealthy father who bought him a very flashy 1947 Pontiac convertible.

Damn, it sounded like fun. But, as I mentioned, I had to work the next day. Saturday in the men's clothing business is usually the busiest day of the week so I had to get some decent sleep.

But the more my friends described the party and even mentioning some of the prettiest girls I knew that would be there etc., the sorrier I felt for myself. "Why can't I go?" I thought to myself. "I'm still young, I can get by with no sleep."

The more pressure my friends put on me, the more I wanted to go. I went back and forth in my head but finally I begged off. I thanked everyone, including Rudy, for the personal invitation but I had to pass.

The next day about 11 a.m. my friend Phil came rushing frantically into the store nearly breathless. He wasn't there to buy anything, but to tell me what had happened the night before and as he talked the color was drained out of his face. He had made a special trip into Manhattan just to tell me that I was "one lucky son of a bitch."

"What do you mean?" I asked worriedly . Then he told me. "Had you gone with Rudy last night you'd probably be dead." "What the hell are you talking about?! I replied, Well, it turns out Rudy and the driver of another car were drag racing on the Belt Parkway at high speed. "What happened?!" I asked worriedly. "Rudy's car lost a wheel," he said somberly.

Evidently the car flipped over a few times. The three people in the back seat were thrown from the car. Rudy was killed instantly and each of the other passengers sustained very serious injuries including concussions, broken bones, internal bleeding, etc. This fellow had just come from the hospital after visiting them. I was shocked and felt terrible for everyone. To think, had I not had to work on Saturday, I could very well have been in that car. Rudy was only twenty-five.

I suppose the moral of this story is, be careful about what you complain about (in this case, my having to work on Saturday) because it might just save your life. Actually another moral is feeling sorry for yourself is a terrible waste of time and energy.

Having lost my dad at age 12 and living through the tough times of the depression, I learned two things: Be grateful for what you have and always be kind to those who have less. As a result of my circumstances, I had "responsibilities" to help my family from an early age. And I think those responsibilities made me a better person.

Much as I might have groused about not going to that party, it was those responsibilities, i.e., work that made me pass on jumping into Rudy's car to go to the party. As I reflect back, I'm pretty certain I never felt sorry for myself again in my life.

CHAPTER 32

NO GOOD DEED GOES UNPUNISHED
(1950)

At work one afternoon a customer came in to try on a suit he had purchased days earlier and had been altered. It fit perfectly and he left seemingly very satisfied. But he was back in the store ten minutes later. I was puzzled. Hopefully, you'll see why.

He explained that while walking past the old Metropolitan Opera House, one of the many birds that sit on a ledge dropped a load of you know what on the shoulder of his overcoat. "Would your tailor remove it, please?" he said matter of factly. I explained that we're not a dry cleaning store, but I would try to see if something could be done.

Reluctantly, I walked into the tailor shop with the man's coat and asked Bill, our presser, if he could remove the bird poop. I explained the man was a customer, so I didn't want to turn him down without making an effort to help. Well, Bill did a good job and removed any trace of what the bird had donated, for lack of a better term.

I handed the coat back to the customer. He put the coat on and didn't think to tip Bill. Ten minutes later, he was back in the store, irate, "I had sixty dollars in my coat pocket and now it's gone!" Oh, brother.

I told the customer that he should have taken the money out of the pocket before he handed me the coat. "Sir, I can't accuse anyone of taking money out of your coat." He got annoyingly angry. "I want to speak to the owner," he insisted.

At that point, I called Wolfgang Kallen to the floor. (We called him "WK.") After I explained what happened to WK, he told the customer the same thing I had. The gentleman (I'm using the term loosely) left in a huff and we should have known that wouldn't be the end of it.

Sure enough, about ten days later we were served with a subpoena to appear in small claims court. You can imagine how mad WK was but there was nothing we could do. On the appointed court date, we rode the subway to city hall station and walked to the court building. We arrived on time and there was the character who summoned us into court.

Just outside the entrance to the courtroom, a man sat at a rectangular table. I guess he was kind of a referee or something. After we told him why we were there he asked the man, who had accused someone in our tailor shop of removing money from his pocket, "What proof do you have?" Well, of course, he had no proof and the case was dismissed right then and there.

We rode back to the store and thought what a waste of time that was. Guess what? Six months later, the same customer was back in the store looking to buy clothing as if nothing had happened. We very politely told him we didn't want his business based on the old expression, "Fool me once shame on you; fool me twice, shame on me." (I can think of another expression that epitomizes my opinion of that customer, but I won't repeat it because this is a PG memoir.)

CHAPTER 33

MOM COULD BE A REGULAR HEDDA HOPPER (1957)

One Saturday afternoon, a customer asked me if I would like two tickets to a world premiere of the biblical epic movie David and Bathsheba, staring Gregory Peck and Susan Hayward. It was to open that night at the Capitol theater at 49th Street and Broadway.

My mother adored Gregory Peck (as many women did) so I gladly took the tickets. I called Mom and she was thrilled. So I told her to take the subway to Manhattan and we could have dinner and then see the premier at the Capitol. So it was, we met at the Hotel Astor lobby at 6:30 that evening.

After dinner, we walked towards the theater. From a block away we could see the Kleig lights shining into the black sky. As we got closer, there were limousines pulling up to the theater as movie stars exited to the flashing lights of photographers cameras. I said, "Mom, we're in for an exciting evening."

We entered the theater and when we got to the lobby, there was a plush red velvet rope separating celebrities from the general public. I realize that the celebrities I'm about to mention, might have no meaning to younger readers. (Under 70!) That said, I hope the gist of the story still comes through.

For example, we saw popular Cuban band leader Xavier Cugat and his then-wife, the voluptuous singer, Abbie Lane. Actresses Polly Bergen and Linda Darnell were there, the latter having won an Academy Award in 1947 for Forever Amber. Also there was actor Red Buttons, who had recently won an Oscar for his role in the 1957 movie Sayonara, starring Marlon Brando.

Mom and I stood behind the ropes until suddenly, and without warning, Mom ducked under and approached Linda Darnell. She just started talking to her as if they were old friends.

I noticed that Mom had a little notebook in her hand and a pen in the other. I thought I'd like to duck under the ropes and was about to do so when an usher caught me in the act. "You can't do that, sir," he said. "But, but..." and I pointed to my mother talking to Linda Darnell. "She's a reporter," he replied.

The truth is Mom has always been fearless and feisty. When she returned to me, Red Buttons passed us and Mom quickly asked him for an autograph. He abruptly turned her down and Mom made it clear she didn't like that one bit. Moments later Buttons was back Apparently, he felt a little guilty.

"OK," he said, "I'll give you my autograph." Mom said, "Never mind. I don't want it. Apparently, since you won the Academy Award, success has gone to your head."

I actually felt a little sorry for Red as now he was pretty much pleading with her to take his autograph. Mom wouldn't have it. Poor Red, he seemed to slink off. Later Mom boasted, "That'll teach him."

CHAPTER 34

ANYBODY GOT CHANGE FOR A GRAND? (1953)

This incident occurred in Kallen's Clothes. About 10:30 in the morning on a weekday, a very distinguished-looking gentleman came into the store with a rather elegant woman. The gentleman asked to see a cashmere overcoat. We rode up to the third floor coat department and about fifteen minutes later I had sold him two cashmere overcoats.

In those days you could buy a good quality, 100% cashmere overcoat made by Jacob Siegal for $235. (In today's terms, that's the equivalent of $2000.) As I totaled the bill I was about to call the fitter because the sleeves needed shortening. "Never mind the alteration," he said. "I'll just take them as they are."

In case you're wondering it's President Grover Cleveland

He then handed me a one thousand dollar bill. I had never seen a thousand-dollar bill before. In fact, I didn't know there was such a thing as a thousand-dollar bill. (Forgive the trivia, but there's actually a $10,000 bill which features the likeness of Salmon P. Chase, Secretary of the Treasury to President Abraham Lincoln.) Back to the story, I looked at the $1,000 bill my customer had handed me and I timidly asked if he had anything smaller and he muttered something under his breath that I couldn't quite make out. I thought the prudent thing to do was to go quickly to the bank and verify the bill wasn't counterfeit.

I took both coats, leaving the customers there on the third floor, explaining that I was going to have the labels removed from the sleeves and also steam out the impressions of the ticket on the fabric. That would give me time to rush to the bank and get back quickly.

I practically ran to the bank and hurried up to the teller.. He examined the bill every which way and confessed that he couldn't be 100% sure whether it was good. Terrific. Not!

I rushed back to the store, rode up to the third floor and explained almost breathlessly to the customer that because it was so early, we hadn't taken enough cash to give him change. At that point, he casually opened his wallet and took out twenties and paid me in full. (Sheesh, why hadn't he done that before?)

You see, when he refused alterations on the sleeves and handed me a thousand dollar bill my suspicions were aroused. It's funny in the retail business, and even in life, the people that seem so suspicious can turn out to be totally honest. Meanwhile, the seemingly nicest customer in the world, can rob the joint blind.

Meanwhile, we rarely ever hear mention of President Cleveland. I hope he appreciates the publicity.

CHAPTER 35

MY GANGSTER "FRIEND" MEETS A BAD END (1954)

To tell this vignette we go back to 1944. As I wrote earlier, Al Glassman and I shared a garden apartment in Waikiki during the twenty-two months I worked as a machinist on Ford Island Naval Air Station in Pearl Harbor. Al and I befriended several guys in the service and told them whenever they spent time in Honolulu they should feel free to make themselves at home in our apartment. There were always plenty of soft drinks in the frig and the key was kept under the doormat. (This seemingly care-free attitude shows you how innocent the world was then.)

One of these soldiers, however, was a questionable character, Murray Aronowitz. Murray was on the short side, though at 5'6," I should talk. However, I was at least two inches taller than Murray, though he was stocky and strong. You wouldn't want to mess with Murray.

One afternoon on my day off, a bunch of servicemen and we civilian Navy Yard workers went to Honolulu Stadium to see a baseball game. Pee Wee Reese, shortstop for the Brooklyn Dodgers, was stationed in Hawaii and playing for the Army as was future Hall of Famer, Johnny Mize. It was a beautiful Sunday and we found good seats in the grandstand. Murray was one of the GIs in our group.

Suddenly, a full Colonel came into the grandstand together with two of his aides. The colonel looked very stiff and full of himself and carried a "swagger stick" under his arm. As they entered the row to their seats, Murray yelled out, "Schmuck!" so loudly you could hear him from fifty yards away.

Everyone else in our group ducked down below our seats to hide. The Colonel and his aides looked up in our direction. It was then that I realized that Murray was a very nervy guy who was liable to do who knew what.

Later, Al reluctantly confided that Murray sold marijuana to some of the GIs on the base. That did it. I told Al that being as how I paid one-half the rent, my one-half said that Murray was barred from coming to our apartment. If ever the police came to our place and caught Aronowitz with pot, we would ALL be in big trouble. (We would lose our jobs and could wind up on the front lines like somewhere in Okinawa.)

About six years later, I was working at Kallen's Clothes when who should come in expressly to see me? None other than Murray Aronowitz who dropped in to buy a suit. Just to make conversation, I asked him what he was doing these days. "I'm in the rackets," he said with considerable braggadocio.

Not long after, I was stunned when I read in the Daily News that Murray had been found slumped over the wheel of his car with a bullet in the back of his head. Murdered gangland style. The article inferred he had been involved in the drug racket and the death was probably "a drug deal gone bad."

Not long after that, I saw another story in the Daily News, The police arrested the man who murdered Murray. You won't believe this, but it was the Colonel whom Murray had called a "schmuck. (I just made that up! Sorry about that, I couldn't help it.)

The actual murderer was a young man in Spanish Harlem and it <u>was</u> a drug deal gone bad. The police had surrounded his apartment building and he gave up without a fight.

Frankly, I could never have imagined Murray coming to such a gruesome ending. On the other hand, all things considered, I wasn't surprised.

CHAPTER 36

TURNS OUT A FEW CUSTOMERS WERE JAILBIRDS (1947-1957)

During the 50 years that I was in the retail men's clothing business, the vast, vast majority of my customers were hard-working, prosperous men. However, I know of 3 (and maybe more) whom I would discover were ex-cons and, I suppose you could say, "current cons" as I will explain.

When I first began working for Kallen's Clothes in March 1947, we had a customer in his 20's who would come in every two months or so. He would always drive a shiny luxury car. I used to wonder how he could afford it on what he earned as an orderly in a Bronx hospital. But as I would learn later from the newspaper account, he had a "side" business.

As the article explained, in hospitals drugs are kept under lock and key and only authorized personnel are allowed access to the cabinet. Somehow, my customer managed to secure a key and suddenly he had his own booming pharmacy business. Eventually, of course he was caught.

The prisons are full of these guys who never thought they would get caught. When they are eventually freed after serving their time, often they say they "Just left the campus," or "the country club." Another one of my other ex-con customers said those exact words when he was released from prison.

Six months earlier, he had purchased a suit, left a deposit and the suit was altered and waiting to be picked up. In the meantime he was in the slammer but we had no idea. In fact, after holding it in the take-out department for one-half year, we put it back in stock. The suit had been altered to fit him, so it wasn't easy to resell. Then one day, two years later (!) he saunters into the store, recognizes me and asks hopefully if I'm still holding the suit.

He was more than a little surprised that we had. He paid the balance and told me he had "Just graduated college." Naive, I almost congratulated him. Lol.

I had a third ex-con as a customer. This particular guy was also built like an Adonis. He kept himself in very good condition; rippling muscles and not an ounce of fat. As I would read in the paper much later here was his modus operandi.

He was a burglar who specialized in fur coats. In this instance, he entered a building that housed numerous fur coat manufacturers. He would go to the men's room and just wait until the wee hours of the morning when nobody was there. He would then break into the factory which would set off the alarm. But, he had his m.o. down so precisely he could get away with it somehow. (Until when he didn't, that is.)

Apparently, he had an incredibly large sack folded and concealed under his coat when he first entered the building. He was able to fill his bag and then climb out the window leading to an alley. He did this before the security company and police arrived.

I don't know how many times he got away with it but, eventually, these guys usually get caught and muscle man was no exception. Knowing him, being in prison gave him plenty of time to do his sit-ups and chin-ups. I never saw him again as by the time he got out, I had moved to Los Angeles.

CHAPTER 37

MY "CAREER"" IN THE NUMBERS RACKET (1957)

One day my boss got a call from an out-of-town department store. The buyer asked Mr. Kallen to gather together all the undesirable merchandise he would like to get rid of, consisting of suits, sports coats, overcoats, topcoats, etc. He said to collect it all together and they would send a truck from Cleveland, to pick up the merchandise and then a check would follow. As instructed, we cobbled together and counted 658 pieces of unwanted merchandise.

The truck driver came into our store and we helped him load the truck. Don't ask me why but as he drove off, I noticed the last 3 numbers of his license plate were 658, the exact number of the garments. What are the odds of that? Oh well.

About an hour later, my boss received a phone call that the deal was off and that the driver would be returning to our store with the 658 garments. My boss was in a bad mood as a result and it wasn't my place to ask him what went wrong.

Actually we workers were in a bad mood, too because now we had wasted our time collecting the garments and now we had to put them back. And even the truck driver seemed crabby as he had to wait for us to unload the garments.

When he finally drove off, once again, I noticed his license plate that ended in 658. It was like haunting me. Now to the meat of the story.

Keep in mind that at that time, the "numbers" racket was huge in New York. It was like the present day lottery only run by the mafia. A couple of guys in the store used to play regularly. In fact, our janitor supplemented his income by being a runner for a "numbers" boss. Up to that day, I never bet on numbers in my life. However, 658 was stuck in my mind.

When I indicated I was going to put two dollars on 658, the other salesmen noticed because it was so out of character for me. All of a sudden we're all pooling our money together and placed $20 on #658.

Well, wouldn't you know, 658 was the winning number and we salesmen went nuts. For our $2 we each got a whopping $375! Everyone thought I was psychic and couldn't wait to play again. It sounds crazy but I had no interest. I only did it that one time because I couldn't not do it, if that makes any sense.

The other guys kept playing the numbers so often they soon lost all their winnings from the one jackpot. They kept asking, "Rosey, what do you think of this number?" They kept thinking I had a special number and was holding out on them. It got tedious to keep denying it.

Yes it was very exciting to have won, but honestly, with the other salesmen always bugging me to come up with another "hot" number, it got to be a royal pain in the butt.

CHAPTER 38

THE REGISTERED LETTER (1959)

My boss at Kallen's Clothes was one of the world's greatest cheapskates. I mean if there was an Olympic Medal for being tight with a buck, he'd win Gold, hands down. But he did recognize my talent and that I did a good job. After 10 years as a salesman I was promoted to store manager. I had learned so much in those years that I was thoroughly up to the task. I don't mean to toot my own horn, but cheap as he was, he knew how effective I was as well.

At this time Kallen's was a much larger store, occupying six floors – four selling floors with offices on the fifth floor and a tailor shop on the sixth floor. The volume of business increased very substantially and I felt I deserved some of the credit. I went three years without a raise and I was going to do something about it. But getting more money out of him was like pulling teeth.

Mr. Kallen probably was thinking: "This kid came to work for me knowing nothing and now he wants more and more money." The fact is, I had built up a good following and other retailers in the neighborhood were frequently making me attractive propositions if I would come to work for them. I had nothing to sell but my time and I wanted to feel appreciated. The way you show appreciation was in the pay envelope.

Mr. Kallen was unbelievably cheap but he wasn't stupid. Quite the contrary. He knew I was due for a raise and, it may sound comical but he was so cheap he became very elusive. I guess his thinking was if I could never get him for 5 minutes he could avoid giving me a raise. Actually, the lengths he went to were comical but I wasn't laughing. I was determined.

It was so ridiculous that if Mr. Kallen found me on the same floor that he was on, he would disappear to another floor. If I was on the second floor and he saw me there, he would immediately leave the floor. As I stated earlier, I could afford to assert myself and be independent knowing I was in demand.

This absurd cat and mouse routine went on for weeks. Finally, I had a brainstorm. Now keep in mind, this was 1959, only about 50 years before "texting" came into existence. What I decided to do was write my boss a registered letter that he would be forced to sign for. In it I explained that I had to resort to sending him a letter because I refused to chase him from floor to floor anymore.

Well, the letter was delivered to him. He had to sign his name showing he had received it. That day, I'll never forget. He came over to me and said, "You write very nice letters," and smiled. I told him that he was the one who forced me to take action by his behavior.

Well, I got my raise and I think he had more respect for me because I showed him I was no pushover.

CHAPTER 39

MOM MEETS JFK... SORT OF (1960)

In 1960, Senator John Kennedy was the Democratic candidate for President running against then Vice-President Richard Nixon. At that time, I was managing Kallen's Clothes. We were located at 474 7th Avenue. A day before the event, I received word that Kennedy was going to speak in front of our store.

There wouldn't be any vehicles allowed to pass through while he was speaking. The campaign didn't have much time left and this was to be a seminal speech. I was an admirer of JFK and Mom was, too. I thought it would be nice if she would come into Manhattan that afternoon, sit at a window where she'd have a great view of the entire proceedings.

When Mom came into the store, I set her up on the fourth floor, and she sat and listened to the entire speech. Afterward she stopped at Dubrow's for a cup of coffee and a Danish. Because it was so crowded, she sat at a table for two, opposite a woman she didn't know.

While sipping coffee, she noticed some unusual activity going on in the cafeteria. Busboys were moving tables, tablecloths were being placed on most of the tables and then they began to bring out big bowls of fruit and baskets with delicious-looking rolls and muffins in them. Mom was a regular at Dubrow's and she could just tell someone important was coming in. But who?

Burning with curiosity, she asked the cashier what was going on. The woman confided that Kennedy was expected to arrive within the hour with an entourage of politicians and an army of reporters. The cashier told Mom not to eat so fast because once she was through and the busboy cleared away the dishes, she'd be asked to leave.

Mom took it all in, returned to the table, and whispered to the woman sitting opposite her that she shouldn't eat too fast. Well, soon Kennedy strode into Dubrow's with his entourage just as the cashier said he would.

He sat down at a table ten feet from Mom. At one point, he looked up from his plate and gave Mom a big smile. What a thrill for her.

Growing up, Mom always lectured me not to eat too fast. And now someone told her to do the same (albeit for different reasons) and as a result, it was one of the most memorable days in her life.

CHAPTER 40

A VACATION THAT WOUND UP FEELING LIKE WORK (1961)

In the summer of 1961, three of my friends and I were able to take a week's vacation together. We were four single guys, longing to breathe fresh air, do some swimming, play some handball and golf and, most importantly, meet girls.

We made reservations at the Neville Hotel in the Adirondack Mountains and gave them a deposit to seal the deal. Thankfully it was small. You'll soon see why I say "thankfully."

We left New York in three cars. I had my car, Mike and his brother Henry, went in their car and Mike Karan, drove his car. We took separate cars so that, if we got "lucky" with the girls, each of us would have his own car to use on the date.

Amazingly, because it was a 4 ½ hour drive from New York, we arrived at the Neville within fifteen minutes of each other. It was the lunch hour, and after checking in, we headed straight for the dining room. Shockingly, however, our waiter was rude to us for "being late to lunch." He then proceeded to share some of the hotel's "rules." Rules? We are on vacation, not in grade school.

After that we all agreed, this was not the place for us. There were a couple of other hotels in the vicinity so, rather than be miserable for a week, we decided to check out the others before we unpacked. Management refused to return our deposit but after that waiter's weird lecture, we were just glad to be out of there, even if we lost the deposit.

We drove around for fifteen minutes until we came upon the very beautiful Lake George. On the other side of the lake was the Hotel Sagamore. The closer we got, the more we realized that this was the hotel for us. Fortunately, they had a room that easily accommodated four people.

It was 2:30 P.M. and we were all a little grimy from the trip. We unpacked and decided to rest up for an hour or two before dinner. After our rest, we got cleaned up and then headed for the dining room. Little did I know what was in store for me.

As the maitre d' was leading us to our table, I heard someone call out my name. It was my boss, Wolfgang Kallen, who was sitting with his wife Mimi and another couple. I must have been in shock at that moment.

"Jerry," he said, "What are you doing here?" I responded somewhat awkwardly, "I'm vacationing for a week." Then I introduced my friends and Wolfgang introduced me to the couple he was sitting with.

On the one hand, I was happy we lucked out by switching hotels but, on the other hand, I was going to be spending a week in the same hotel with my boss so I'd have to be careful about every move I made. Yikes!

Mimi, was one of the most charming and attractive women you could ever hope to meet. As it turned out, my boss was not a dancer, so I asked her to dance when it was appropriate. I was in an awkward position but I made the best of it and managed to have a great time.

However, That first night in the dining room after the introductions were over, Wolfgang turned to his rich friend and said, "You see, Harry, I pay my people so well they can afford to take a vacation in the same hotels as us."

CHAPTER 41

CHATTING WITH A PULITZER PRIZE WINNER (1962)

In the spring of 1962, I took my mother to see a Broadway musical, Fiorello, based on the life of the former and fabled Mayor of New York City, Fiorello H. La Guardia. He was a colorful character and some of the old timers who lived through the Depression remember him well—and I'm one of them.

We were enjoying the show and, during the intermission, we remained in our seats. Only days before I had been watching David Susskind's weekly TV program The Round Table. A group of people would sit around a table and discuss all sorts of interesting topics. There would be a few regulars and then there were highly intelligent guests who would contribute to the discussion.

The guests varied from week to week and David Susskind was the very skilled moderator. As I sat there, in the theater, during intermission, I inadvertently turned around to see who was sitting behind me. It was none other than the man who wrote Fiorello, Jerome Weidman! I recognized him immediately, having seen him on the Susskind show only days earlier.

Don't ask me where I got the chutzpah, but I casually introduced myself. I told him how much I was enjoying the play and mentioned that Mom was too. "Yes," he said. "My mother likes it as well."

The show was actually terrific. In fact, it eventually won a Pulitzer Prize for Drama for Mr. Weidman. However, my curiosity got the better of me, which I confess has happened to me for good and ill throughout my life. (Hopefully mostly for good.) I had to ask Mr. Weidman, "Considering the show has been playing for months, why are you here now?"

He answered as though we were old friends. "I like to come back, now and then, to make sure they're doing it right." He then introduced me to his wife and asked if Mom and I would like to join them for a drink after the show at Sardi's Restaurant, across the street from the theater.

I truly hated to do it, but I had to beg off. I politely explained that I had to get up early the next morning because I had to be at work at 9:00 A.M. and we still had to take a subway all the way to the last stop at Brighton Beach. I was managing the Kallen store at the time and we had a full staff who were counting on me to open the store on time. Again, I thanked him for the lovely invitation and we each went our separate ways.

I wonder sometimes if I had accepted his offer, what could have followed. Who knows?

Maybe I would have become a friend? We were both New Yorkers and relatively around the same age. (He was 10 years older but he looked much younger.)

Laguardia, New York's 99th Mayor. (And worst airport!)

Sadly, in 1998, I read in the obituary section of the LA Times that he had passed away. He had written 20 novels, 10 short stories, 5 Broadway plays, and 8 movies. Not only was he so talented and prolific, but he was quite a gentleman. One thing's for sure, he's the only Pulitzer Prize winner I'd ever chatted with. (That is, so far)

CHAPTER 42

I DIDN'T GO IN SPACE, BUT I KNEW TWO WHO DID (1962 & 1969)

On October 4, 1957, at the height of the Cold War, the Russians shocked the world when they launched the Sputnik satellite into an elliptical low Earth orbit. It was viewed in the U.S. as a crisis, especially when Sputnik orbited for three weeks. America went into a scientific panic as we were clearly years behind the Russians. But it only got worse.

In 1959, Russian cosmonaut Yuri Gagarin, was the first person to orbit the earth. However, in January, 1961, JFK began his presidency and, on May 25, 1961, in an urgent speech to Joint session of Congress, he vowed, "I believe that this nation should commit itself to achieving the goal, before this decade is out, of landing a man on the Moon and returning him safely to earth." (Spoiler alert: we did it!)

In 1962, we had advanced to the point we could attempt to send astronaut Colonel John Glenn up in space with the hopes he could orbit the earth. Millions of Americans, including yours truly, were on pins and needles. Little did I know one day I would be selling clothes to Colonel Glenn. But once again, I don't want to get ahead of myself.

While Glenn's capsule was being launched I was working in Kallen's Clothes in Manhattan but I was also riveted by Glenn's upcoming flight. I constantly checked my transistor radio for updates on the flight, praying it would be a success. And when it was successful, the country celebrated Glenn's heroic feat like it was a national holiday. Suddenly, the space race was in full gear.

I relocated to Los Angeles in 1963. Finally, in 1969, we sent men to the moon—a major event in the history of man. That year, I was working for Snyder & Son in the Century Plaza Hotel in Century City. The city planned a big reception that evening in our hotel for all the astronauts. That afternoon, guess who came walking into our store? Colonel John Glenn and his wife, Annie!

"I need a white dinner jacket and formal pants," Glenn said with some urgency. I was thrilled. I sat Annie in a comfortable chair, found a dinner jacket and pants for the Colonel, and had it ready in plenty of time for the reception. It was an honor to wait on Colonel Glenn who radiated strength and grace.

Now, fast forward to 1982. I'm working for Mike Caruso the leading men's clothing store in Santa Monica. A man came in and asked me to measure him for a made-to-measure tuxedo. In our conversation he somehow mentioned that he wanted to go up in space as a civilian. (Trust me, that was not exactly a conversation I had with any other customer, ever.)

His name was Dennis Tito who was extremely wealthy. In fact, it was reported all over the country that he had offered twenty million dollars if NASA would send him into space. But for some reason, NASA turned him down so, instead, he offered the same twenty million to the Russians and they accepted. Fairly soon thereafter, Mr. Tito went up in space, just like Colonel Glenn, but without the fanfare.

So, here's Jerry Rosenblum, born in Brooklyn to working class, immigrant parents, with only a high school education, who waited on the first American to orbit earth, Colonel John Glenn, and also waited on the first "civilian" to orbit the earth, Dennis Tito. Only in America.

CHAPTER 43

GO WEST YOUNG MAN, ONLY I WASN'T THAT YOUNG (1963)

The main reason I moved to Los Angeles was because Mom's doctor advised me that it would add ten years to her life if we moved to a mild climate. (To be technical, it may have added 37 years as she lived to 102.) She was 65 and couldn't take the intensely cold winters and the hot and humid summers. Florida was ruled out because of the sweltering summer months.

I gave some thought to Honolulu where I had lived for two years during World War II. However, when I discovered the pay scale was considerably lower than it was in New York, I ruled out Hawaii. Fortunately, just when I needed it, an opportunity presented itself.

As fate would have it, the national sales manager of Botany 500 paid us a visit one afternoon. I mentioned to him that I was very seriously thinking of relocating to an area with a mild climate—and I explained why.

"Jerry," he said. "Botany just bought a chain of men's clothing stores in Los Angeles. You could work there as a manager of one of the stores." I had never been to Los Angeles, but I had heard people used to refer to it as "God's country." (In 2019, with the horrific traffic jams, if it's God's country it means He has a strange sense of humor.)

"Here's what you do," he told me. "Call Mr. Mike Fineman. He's the merchandise manager for three men's clothing chains that Botany owns here in New York. He will interview you. If he likes you, he will bring you into Mr. Ralph Schneider's office for final approval. If everything turns out satisfactory, you'll be on your way."

I went home that night and discussed it with Mom. This was a very important decision for both of us. Except for two years in Hawaii, I had never lived anywhere but New York. It would mean I would be 3000 miles away from my younger brother, Artie and his wife, Ronnie, and their two children, Mark and Heidi. But I figured that once we got established, we could always fly back for a visit, perhaps yearly. Or, who knows, maybe they would eventually move to L.A.

Also, I would be giving up a job in a store where I had been working for sixteen years. I knew what I had but I didn't know what I would be getting in to. "What if things don't work out? What then?"

As I think back, I realize that I had a lot of confidence in myself and guts, too. I knew the business because I had learned from experts. I had gone as far in Kallen's Clothes as I was going to get. So, as I often say, "Nothing ventured, nothing gained."

I went for the interviews and I could see I made a very good impression on both men. The offer was made and I accepted. I was on my way. I sold my furniture, gave notice to the landlord and we said our good-byes to the family and friends.

Mr. Kallen was so shocked I was leaving I began to think that I was taking too big of a chance, but my mind was made up. I was given a "going away" party at a restaurant, Bill Bertelotti's in Greenwich Village, which was owned by a customer of ours.

So there we were, my mother and I in a Pan Am jet heading to the city of Angels. During the flight my mother took a nap. As I looked at her, a wave came over me, not that I didn't already know, but that this was a huge move.

Let's face it, my mother had no friends in L.A., she didn't have any doctors lined up and we didn't know where we'd be living. The truth is there would be so many difficult adjustments and all I could do was hope that they would work out in time.

At that moment I felt more responsible for her than even when I was 12 and hustling dimes and quarters delivering drug store prescriptions. Suddenly I found myself thinking about my father who passed away almost 30 years earlier. What would he think of what I was doing? Would he proud of me? Or would he be worried? I felt a tinge of "I wish he were here to help, to assure me everything was going to work out fine." (Actually, maybe more than a tinge.)

My reverie was interrupted by an attractive stewardess who offered me a complimentary margarita. I took a few sips and my doubts seemed to evaporate with each additional sip. The fact is, however, all my life, once I set my mind to do something, I always saw it through and I just made it work. And Mom was a smart, practical woman who remarkably stretched dollars during the Depression so that we survived. We were going to be just fine in L.A.

Our car was being driven out to meet us. The driver asked that we stay a few days at the Biltmore Hotel as he was familiar with it and it would make the transfer simpler. So Mom and I checked into the Biltmore. After we got settled we walked to a Los Angels landmark, Pershing Square.

As we sat down on a nice bench the view of downtown Los Angeles was impressive. The many benches were occupied by homeless people who were using them to sleep on. That was a little disconcerting. Then clouds rolled in and it started to drizzle. Mom turned to me and said half-jokingly, "So this is Los Angeles?" We both had a good laugh.

The next day the gentleman who drove our car, a 1962 Chevy Impala, four-door, across country arrived ahead of schedule at the Biltmore. He turned over the car. we signed some papers and he was off. And Mom and I were going to take our first drive in L.A.

So there we were driving down the world-famous Wilshire Boulevard heading west, hoping to find an affordable furnished apartment. Don't ask me how or why, something told me to stop at a newsstand. (And it definitely wasn't to get a paper!) I explained to the owner of the stand, I was looking for an apartment to which he immediately closed his newsstand and said, "Come with me."

We walked two and half blocks to Detroit Street. He took us into an apartment building and introduced us to the building manager who proceeded to show us a furnished apartment that suited us nicely and we rented it. Just like that.

As fate would have it, the Harris & Frank store I was to manage was only two and a half blocks from where we would now be living. I could walk to work. I hadn't had it this convenient since I was 14 and working for Mr. Weiner at the drugstore! Yes, gang, things were starting to work out.

CHAPTER 44

SAVING A SINKING SHIP (1963)

The store I was to manage was one of the oldest in the Harris & Frank chain and had one more year on a five-year lease but business had been going steadily downhill. I gathered the former manager used to hang out in the bar next to the store and, as a result, did a poor job of managing . (But probably a decent job of staying drunk.)

I remember the superintendent of operations of this 23-store chain asking me what I intended to do in order to get customers in. I pointed to a sixteen-story office building directly across the street and predicted that a lot of the business would be coming out of that building.

Every morning before I opened the store, I stopped in the lobby of Lee Tower, the office building across the street. From the directory I copied the names of businesses and the executives who headed the companies. Later I would call "information," get their phone number and make my cold calls. ("Jerry Rule #1," You can't be an introvert and be a successful salesman.)

I explained that I was the new manager of the Harris & Frank store and would like to get acquainted. I offered various "free services," like, if they have a business meeting to attend and they need their suit pressed, we would be of service at no charge. Or, if a button had to be replaced on a jacket or pant, we would gladly do it.

Gradually, traffic started to increase and by the end of the first year, business was up $50,000. Based on that strength, the lease was renewed for another five years. The second year we beat the previous year by another $50,000. In 20+ years on the east coast, I had made a name for myself, now, in just two years, I had done the same on the west. Next, I would conquer the world! (Sorry about that, I just got carried away.)

CHAPTER 45

CESAR: ET TU, JERRY? (1964)

This chapter will take us back in time. Cesar Romero was a very handsome, leading man actor who was quite popular in the '30s through the '60s. In 1944, I remember seeing Romero in Honolulu. He was a seaman in the Coast Guard and, one Sunday, my friends and I went to the Waikiki Steak House. The specialty was filet mignon where we saw Romero there with some of his shipmates.

After the war, Romero continued to make movies and, in between films, he became a goodwill ambassador for Petrocelli Clothes. He stood six foot three, had a very good build and a thick head of wavy hair that women adored. When Cesar smiled, he had pearly white teeth that looked like Chiclets.

Our store, Kallen's Clothes, was the biggest account that Petrocelli had and it was decided that Cesar should make a guest appearance in our store. We posted a sign on the front door telling the public that Cesar Romero would be here at 1 pm. Sure enough, promptly at 1 pm, a large stretch limo pulled up right in front and out stepped Cesar Romero.

Romero was born in Cuba and spoke Spanish fluently. At the time of his appearance at our store, there were lots of Spanish-speaking people working in the Garment District. When his limo parked in front of the store and Cesar stepped out, it was a big event in their lives, especially when Cesar spoke to them in Spanish.

We had a table of hors d'oeuvres and drinks and he mingled and signed autographs. After about a half hour of this, he turned to me and asked, "Jerry, is there a chair handy so I can sit down? I'm not as young as I used to be."

Just then, a photographer hired by Petrocelli,t called out, "Jerry, I want to take a picture of you with Cesar." I agreed, reluctantly, thinking to myself how was I going to look standing next to a tall, handsome hunk like Cesar Romero?

We stood next to each other. He had a big smile and showed those white "Chiclets" teeth. I looked like a proverbial deer in the headlights. Now we fast forward two years.

In 1964, I was living in L.A. and managing a Harris & Frank store. I was asked by the president to go to the Biltmore Hotel downtown. They were having a men's clothing convention at the hotel that weekend and Cesar Romero would be in the room rented by Petrocelli Clothes.

Romero was there to greet his fans and the retailers selling Petrocelli clothes. I took Mom with me, figuring it would be a thrill for her to meet Cesar Romero. Not only did she get to meet him, she took a picture with him and so did I. Fast forward 25 years!

Too bad Romero wasn't handsome.

In 1989, I was working at Mike Caruso in Santa Monica. We had a sweater in the window that attracted—you guessed it—Cesar Romero. When he came in, I was taking care of another customer so one of the other salesmen found the sweater he wanted. By that time, I had finished with my customer. He and I and other salesmen on the floor crowded around Cesar as his sale was being written up. And I thought I'd have some fun with him.

"Cesar," I said, "don't you remember me?" I could read his mind. "Now who the hell is this guy?" I said, "Cesar, we were in a couple of pictures together." "We were?" he replied thinking I had meant movies. I then explained what kind of "pictures" I was talking about.

"Wise guy!" he said turning to the other salesmen. He was right about that, and everybody had a good laugh.

CHAPTER 46

THE BEST LUCK IS WHAT YOU MAKE YOURSELF (1965)

While business at my store was steadily improving, the Harris & Frank store in Santa Monica was in decline. The owners hoped if they brought me to Santa Monica maybe I could capture lightning in a bottle. When you work for a chain you have no say in the matter. (Like a highly paid professional athlete except you're certainly not remotely that highly paid, trust me.)

After working in Santa Monica for 6 months, Maury Mandel, the president of Mullen & Bluett, another men's clothing chain, came into the store one morning. Very discreetly he said that he'd like to see me on my day off as he had an "interesting proposition."

Intrigued, I went to see him. To my surprise, he offered me the manager's position of the flagship store of the Mullen & Bluett chain whose manager had died three weeks earlier from a sudden heart attack. I would be earning considerably more than Harris & Frank was paying me.

I thought the fair thing was to go to Mike Fineman, the president of Harris & Frank, and see if he could match that figure. But Fineman politely said no deal. So I took the new job as manager of the main store of Mullen & Bluett. I was definitely moving up the ladder.

Not only was the money considerably better, the new store was only a few blocks from where I lived. Now I had six clothing salesmen, four sales people and an assistant manager.

I managed Mullen & Bluett 1965-68

The first full year with Mullen & Bluett was the best in the history of the store. I remember Maury Mandel putting his arm on my shoulder and telling me, "Jerry, you must have come here with a horseshoe in your pocket." Somehow I didn't entirely trust him. As you will soon see, I had good reason.

CHAPTER 47

THE PERNICIOUS PERKS OF POLITICIANS (1968)

In the 1940's and 50's it seemed like almost every man took pride in his clothes. And, thankfully for me and my colleagues, business was great. In the 1960's many men seem to have less concern with their clothes to the point jeans T-shirts were standard fare for many. Naturally this adversely affected business. Not only that but at Mullen & Bluett we had lots of competition.

Next door, was Phelps Turkel. Close by was Harris & Frank, Silverwoods, Desmonds, the Broadway and Orbach's—all within the bounds of our store. So we had to work even harder to get business and we did.

Under my guidance, our store did the biggest business in menswear of all the stores in the area. If we ran a sale, people knew it was a legitimate sale. The markdowns we offered really brought in the traffic. On a typical, busy Saturday afternoon, all seven of our steady clothing salesmen did very well.

We had a room next to the sales floor designated as the fitting room. After a customer put on his new suit, he would then leave one of the dressing rooms (we had ten) and proceed to the fitting room where his salesman waited with the fitter. After the garment was fitted, the customer would change back into the clothes he wore into the store.

On this particularly busy Saturday afternoon, one of the salesmen whispered that his customer claimed that sixty-four dollars had been removed from his wallet in the dressing room.

Keep in mind, we had a sign in each dressing room asking people not to leave valuables in the dressing room and to make sure as they leave they close the door, which automatically locked it. We took these precautions knowing that, on a very busy day, a professional thief might want to take advantage.

The customer in question was Los Angeles County Supervisor, Kenneth Hahn. He explained that the money was removed from his wallet but everything else was intact. Now, normally, I might have pointed out, given the sign, that we weren't responsible. But I certainly wasn't going to tell that to Supervisor Hahn. (By the way, his son became mayor of Los Angeles, twenty-five years later.)

So, I opened the cash register and handed Supervisor Hahn sixty-four dollars with an apology. That Monday, I explained to our CEO what had happened and, to my relief, he said I had done the right thing.

The following Saturday, it happened again only it was $50 supposedly taken. This time, however, I pointed out to the customer that he had been careless about leaving valuables in the dressing room and not locking the door. While not exactly thrilled, he understood.

After he left, I went next door to Phelps Terkel, to ask whether they had had a similar experience. No, it hadn't happened in their store. However, they thanked me for alerting them.

I was starting to get suspicious about one of our clothing salesmen. He was a horse player and I thought maybe he may have had some losses and needed money, but I didn't dare accuse him. He was a married man with two teenage children and I had absolutely no proof.

Thankfully, it didn't happen again and I was so relieved. Things were hectic enough and I didn't need the extra aggravation. I suppose one advantage of today's jeans and t-shirt society, you don't need a lot of dressing rooms.

CHAPTER 48

MY VACATION CROSSED PATHS WITH HISTORY (1968)

This chapter took place in 1968 when I took a vacation in Hawaii. I decided to take Mom with me so she could see where I spent nearly two years of my life, during WWII. A limousine transported us from the airport to the Royal Hawaiian Hotel.

As we headed toward Waikiki, newsboys were holding up newspapers announcing in bold type that President Lyndon Johnson was due that day. He arrived at the Royal Hawaiian at just about the same time we did and he was staying at the Royal Hawaiian, too. Frankly, it was pretty exciting to have the POTUS staying under the same roof as us.

President Johnson was there for a meeting with President Nguyen Van Thieu of South Vietnam to discuss how to find peace and end the war. Many members of the President's cabinet were there too—Secretary of State Dean Rusk, Secretary of Defense Robert McNamara, Ambassador Averell Harriman, Adviser McGeorge Bundy, and Johnson's press secretary, Bill Moyers.

The networks also sent their top correspondents, including Harry Reasoner. I had planned to take Mom sightseeing, but how could we leave the hotel with all the excitement going on? Naturally, Secret Service men were all over the place.

Suddenly, word circulated that the President would be passing through the hotel corridor where we were standing. Sure enough, only minutes later, he had one Secret Service man in front, one on each side and one in back, all of them wearing a small hearing device in their ear.

At one point, I passed a room that had been converted to a press room. I looked in and saw Bill Moyers on a platform reporting on what was happening. Security was only admitting members of the press. Frankly, I wanted to go inside, too. I had a Kodak camera hanging from my neck and it occurred to me that if I posed as a reporter I might be able to walk into the press room, just like I belonged.

That is exactly what I did. I walked in, right past the guard who evidently took me for a reporter. I found myself standing near Harry Reasoner and next to McGeorge Bundy.

I stood there for about fifteen minutes and decided not to "press" my luck. (Pun intended.) I left before anyone realized I didn't belong there. With all the prominent people there I felt like I was seeing history in the making. After they left Hawaii, Mom and I got in our sightseeing and had a memorable vacation.

About ten years later, I was watching a shuffleboard game at the courts in Santa Monica when I saw three men approaching from the distance. One had a tripod camera over his shoulder, and another carried a traveling bag and sound equipment. The third man was Bill Moyers!

They stopped at the court and Moyers asked me if anything exciting was going on. I told him the two men playing were in their nineties: one was 97 and the other was 92. Moyers told his assistants to set up the cameras to photograph the game. I remember him saying, "We still have a little film left in the camera."

As they were filming, I told Mr. Moyers, "Bill," I said, "this is the second time I've been this close to you." "Really?" he said. "When was the first time?" "The Honolulu Conference at the Royal Hawaiian Hotel with Johnson and Thieu, ten years ago." "Were you there, too?" he asked.

Not long after that incident and shortly after we finally extricated ourselves from South Vietnam, I was working at the Century Plaza Hotel. One day, three men came walking into the store. The man in the center was ex-President Thieu and two Secret Service men were accompanying him.

I said to Thieu, "Sir, this is the second time I've been this close to you." "Really? When was the first time?" "The Honolulu Conference at the Royal Hawaiian Hotel when you met with President Johnson." "Were you there, too?" he asked. He was even more surprised than Moyers.

As for my running into famous people like this, my writer friend, Jack, calls me the "Thinking man's Forest Gump." (I hope that's a compliment.) I don't really know how I manage to cross paths with these folks, sometimes decades between encounters. All I can say, it's kind of the story of my life. Or one of them.

CHAPTER 49

GETTING A PINK SLIP STINKS! (1968)

Remember when I said I didn't entirely trust my boss? Well, four months after my Hawaii vacation, I was in for a very unpleasant surprise, one like I'd never had in my life.

The Mullen & Bluett chain was owned by B.V.D. Underwear with corporate offices in New York. One day, the comptroller of B.V.D. flew out to visit some of the stores in our chain. To my chagrin, he asked why business had fallen off. I told him, "If I knew the answer to that question I probably would be in President Johnson's cabinet."

After he left, I remember Maury Mandel joked about my recent vacation, "Jerry, if things don't pick up around here we might have to give you a permanent vacation." Moments later he said he was only kidding. Some jokester, huh? Not! Obviously I didn't take too kindly to an intimation of being fired. And yet, so it was months later, I was given a pink slip as manager. No fun at all!

Here's what happened. Mullen & Bluett was bought out by a northern California clothing retail chain. And soon they began cost cutting. When they saw my manager's salary, they balked. And shortly thereafter, you could say I was toast. (Actually, I like toast, so I don't know why people use that term, but, then again, I just did.)

So here I had gone from top dog to the dog house. I was offered a job as a salesman, which I'm glad I had the integrity to pass on. The truth is it was a blow to my ego and my lifelong work ethic. Put it this way, from the age of 12, until now, I had been "unemployed" for a total of two weeks. So I wasn't going to take this lying down. (Although as I'm editing this memoir, I'm actually lying down.)

I immediately spread the word in the "business" I was on the market. It wasn't exactly like today's "going viral," on social media, but it was creating activity on what we called the grapevine. Sure enough, within two weeks, bingo, I got a call from from Bob Snyder who owned Snyder & Sons in the Century Plaza Hotel.

The interview went so well, Bob and his dad, Billy Snyder, asked how soon could I start. This was November 5th, 1968, election day. Richard Nixon became our new President and I began as the new salesman at Snyder & Son at the Century Plaza Hotel. (Suffice it to say, I lasted in my job longer than Nixon did in his.)

Almost from that very day, I found working in the hotel shop a distinct pleasure. I was dealing with a very successful clientele—CEO types and notable people from the entertainment industry, who worked in front of and behind the camera. Our customers consisted of politicians, well-known sports figures and even underworld characters.

The best years of my working life.

And guess what gang, after working there only one year, I was promoted to manager, proving you can't keep a good man down, or at least not this good man. Anyway, I did feel vindicated but I didn't let it go to my head, it just felt good in the self esteem department.

I truly believe that success comes only if you're willing to do the hard work. I'd been doing since I was 12. It was long ago in my DNA and, again, it paid off in the end. But enough of "Jerry's keys to success," as this is starting to sound like an infomercial.

CHAPTER 50

TURN ON THE BUBBLE MACHINE (1969)

In 1969, one of my Mullen & Bluett salesman brought over a customer to meet me. "Jerry, I'd like to introduce you to Mr. Bradshaw. He's an executive with the Lawrence Welk Show." Mr. Bradshaw and I chatted for a few minutes about Welk when he volunteered, "Say Jerry, would you like two tickets to the show?" "Absolutely. I'm a big fan and so is my mother."

Just like that, Mr. Bradshaw handed me tickets for the upcoming Sunday show. I placed them in my wallet and thanked him. When I came home that night I told Mom and I could see that it made her day.

Well, Sunday came and we drove to the ABC Theater in Hollywood. I remember just glancing at the tickets before we left but not reading the fine print. Uh oh.

You see, the tickets read that the doors open at 3:30 P.M. but suggested people line up in front of the theater at 2:45. So that explained why we were last in line. Mom was perturbed, realizing we would likely end up in the balcony in the last row.

And that's exactly where we ended up. And even worse, we had a pillar in front of us partially blocking our view. Just then, an usher beckoned me and Mom to follow him. He led us downstairs and placed us in the first row orchestra. It took me a few minutes but I finally figured out why.

You see, this was going to be Lawrence Welk's very first color broadcast. Most of the people who stood in line in front of us were dressed very casually, wearing tank tops, t-shirts and jeans or walking shorts. Mom and I were actually dressed up as befitting the occasion. I wore a sport coat and slacks with a shirt and tie. Mom, who was always concerned about her appearance, wore a nice-looking suit ensemble with a coordinating blouse.

In fact, we were probably the best-dressed people in the audience. When the cameraman panned the audience, the producer probably wanted to show as many people as possible who were dressed appropriately. As soon as we got settled in our seats, out from behind the curtain Lawrence Welk stepped out onto the stage. He announced that he would be asking some of the ladies in the audience to dance with him.

Mom sprung right into action. Out came the make-up kit, mirror, lipstick, comb, etc. And sure enough, Mom was the first one to be called to the stage by Welk. She was so excited that, instead of asking me to watch her purse, she asked the man who sat to her left, a complete stranger!

Mom danced for about fifteen seconds, then a woman tapped her on her shoulder and that meant that it was her turn to dance. So, on and on it went until all the ladies that had assembled had gotten their turn to dance.

I was so happy for Mom. It gave her so much joy she had actually danced with someone she admired so much. Also, even though I had goofed by not reading the tickets, it meant that I wouldn't come home to a cold supper.

CHAPTER 51

WHAT THE WELL DRESSED MURDERER SHOULD WEAR (1971)

In 1985 there was a brutal murder of an elderly Jewish couple, Gerald and Vera Woodman. that rocked the city of Los Angeles, especially the tight knit Jewish community. It wasn't as big as O.J. Simpson or the Menendez brothers' murders that would follow, but at the time, it grabbed the attention of all of Southern California and even much of the nation. (The story was so compelling that Larry Attebury, the news anchor on KTTV, Channel 11, wrote a book about this case, Flesh and Blood.

The retired couple were killed by gunfire in the garage of their condo as they arrived home from a festive meal at the conclusion of the Jewish holy day of Yom Kippur. The press dubbed the crimes the "Ninja murders," because the killer was described as wearing a black ninja costume. (In reality, it was just a hoodie.)

It was in the early '70s, when I first saw Stewart. He was 21 when he came into the store one day to buy some clothing where I was working at Snyder & Son at the Century Plaza Hotel. We assigned Billy Snyder's stepson to wait on him because they were about the same age. Sure enough, Stewart became a regular customer.

A couple of years went by and I remember he came into the store with a big dog. While Stewart was looking around, the dog lifted his hind leg and peed all over a display. I thought Billy would have a stroke. To his credit, Stewart immediately paid for the merchandise that was ruined. (Not that he had much choice.)

Stewart came from a well-to-do family. His father was an English Jew who came to the United States after WWII and went into business for himself. He had two sons and a daughter. He was happily married with a devoted wife and lived in a condominium in Brentwood. He manufactured fixtures meant for kitchen cabinets.

Older brother Neil and Stewart were learning the business and would eventually take over when their father retired. However, the father was a harsh taskmaster and was very controlling of the two boys. It was his way or the highway.

Both brothers married and began to raise their own families. Everyone, including the Woodman parents, would get together on birthdays, holidays, and special occasions. All this while, the two sons, Neil and Stewart, were learning the business and gradually taking over from their father. Unfortunately, they also acquired a gambling habit and would go to Las Vegas, whenever they could.

They were degenerate gamblers and they would lose much more than they would win.

Even worse, the sons owed a lot to loan sharks and needed money to meet their payroll. Also, if they didn't come up with half a million dollars real quick, they stood the chance of getting killed. They were desperate.

Spoiler alert, both brothers arranged for a couple of contract killers, to murder their father to get their $500,000 inheritance. The murders were to be on Yom Kipper day, around 5:00 P.M. when he would be driving into his garage with his wife and they could make it look like a holdup that had gone wrong. Not exactly what you'd call a "close knit family."

Apparently the Woodman brothers forgot "Honor Thy Mother & Father."

With skillful detective work, the police figured out what had happened. As if the story needed more weirdness, the hitman was Steven Homick, a former LAPD cop!

He was assisted by his brother, Robert Homick, a westside attorney. (Good Lord!) Steven was sentenced to death but died on death row of natural causes in 2014. Robert was given a life sentence.

Stewart received a life sentence only escaping the death penalty by agreeing to testify against Neil. Curiously, Neil also died in prison of natural causes in 2014.

After the murder, I read that Stewart's wife went to work selling cars at Martin Cadillac at Bundy Drive and Olympic Boulevard. Both wives eventually divorced their husbands and may have remarried by now.

The whole thing is so gruesome, two brothers hiring two other brothers to brutally kill their parents. Not exactly the stuff of a Broadway musical. Although, these days, who knows.

CHAPTER 52

EXCUSE ME, BUT SHOULDN'T YOU BE IN JAIL? (1972)

In 1973, in Los Angeles, a huge corporate scandal was revealed when the whistle was blown on Equity Funding, for massive accounting fraud, including a computer system dedicated to creating and maintaining fictitious insurance policies. The CEO was Stanley Goldblum and the CFO (chief financial officer) was Fred Levin.

Goldblum was convicted and sentenced to eight years in prison whereas Levin was sentenced to seven. I remember all of this only because it had to do with one of our customers at Snyder & Son.

Jerry Blauner, a man who made his fortune in scrap metal, was a good customer of ours. One Saturday morning, he came into the store with a man and he wanted me to sell his friend a tuxedo. As it turned out, the man wore a size 46 regular and we didn't have his size in the style he wanted. I said I could order it first thing Monday and have it sent to the store. It was agreed that's what we would do.

Blauner's friend looked familiar to me for a good reason. It was Fred Levin, the former CFO of Equity Funding! I thought he was supposed to be in jail. What was he doing walking around looking at clothing? He looked nice and tan like he had been on a two-week cruise to the Caribbean.

Monday, I ordered the tuxedo and shortly after that I received a phone call from Blauner. He asked if I had ordered the tux. I said, "Yes." "Cancel it," he said. "Over the weekend, I received a call from the Chabad."

It seemed that Blauner and Levin were planning some sort of business together. Jerry was to put up the money for offices in Westwood. He told me that after receiving the phone call he was told who this guy Levin really was.

Levin was incarcerated in a prison in the San Diego area dubbed "Club Fed." Because he was a white-collar criminal, during the week he put in his time and was let out on the weekends. Club Fed has a fitness center, swimming, tennis, and country club atmosphere. Ivan Boesky, another greedy SOB, stayed there, too.

So the deal was called off and Blauner lost several thousand dollars as a result. Blauner regularly contributed to Chabad and in appreciation for his generosity, they tipped him off about Levin. As for Club Fed, with all the amenities, it sounds so lovely I'm tempted to ask where do I sign up?

CHAPTER 53

I FELT LIKE NOAH, ONLY WETTER (1972)

We've all heard the expression "Expect the unexpected." One day at Snyder & Son, I was waiting on a customer when the man's friend pointed to the ceiling. "I think you guys have a leak." Sure enough, he was right.

Water began to drip from the ceiling in two or three places. I excused myself and ran for a receptacle to catch the water. By then, water was literally pouring down from the ceiling from a half-dozen places. I shut off all the lights and all the salespeople started to pick up handfuls of clothing bringing it to the back stockroom away from the water.

I called maintenance to find out what was going on. You see, our store was located directly under the hotel's executive offices. A plumber, I was told, had screwed up and caused the problem. Billy Snyder, my boss's father, had gone to lunch about five minutes before this happened.

Thank God, I remembered to salvage a tuxedo. I had special ordered for the owner of the twin movie theaters that were scheduled to open that night across the street at the new ABC Entertainment Center. The Plitt Theaters were part of a chain of theaters owned by Mr. Plitt and the tuxedo was for the grand opening.

There was to be a cocktail party in the hotel before the movie. That night was the world premiere of the movie Cabaret starring Liza Minnelli. In fact, the vice president of ABC, in charge of real estate, had given me a ticket which entitled me to go to the cocktail party and the movie, as well.

When Billy Snyder returned to the store he was in shock. He had left forty-five minutes before and everything was running smoothly and now he looked as pale as a ghost as he asked, "What the hell happened!?" I remember putting my arm around his shoulder explaining that it could be a blessing in disguise.

"We've got some merchandise in the store that we haven't been able to move in a couple years. Fortunately, it got soaked. The insurance company will make good on all of it and the carpet, too." We then called the fire department who pumped out the water. We had to take up all the carpeting and struggled along on bare cement for two weeks until the new carpet was laid.

Oh yes, something else I remember that happened at the height of all this excitement—one of the guests of the hotel came into the store. We had no lights and our staff was scurrying back and forth trying to save merchandise. Billy Snyder and I were standing near the entrance when he entered and said, "There's a pair of shoes in the display case. Do you have that shoe in my size?"

Billy told him, "This is a disaster area, sorry we can't help you at this time." The guest persisted, "But I'm checking out of the hotel this afternoon so could you please look for the shoe?" Generally "the customer is always right," but not in this case.

The insurance company sent a representative to appraise all the damage and a nice check came in the mail shortly after that. You could say it all came out in the wash. (If you're groaning now, sorry about that.)

CHAPTER 54

THE CLOSEST I CAME TO AN OSCAR
(1972)

When I was ten years old, I had a terrific 4th grade teacher, Daniel Fuchs who was in his early 20's and was a God to us kids. The school was P.S. 225 in Brighton Beach. This was 1932 and a public school teacher didn't make much money. (Actually, they really still don't but that's another story.)

To supplement his income, Mr. Fuchs would write love stories for the pulp magazines. They were popular because people could forget their troubles reading that type of fiction. The country was in a very severe depression and people needed escapist entertainment. Of course, it was way before television.

So, I remember Mr. Fuchs, especially when he explained that he was leaving for the West Coast. Warner Bros. Studios had signed him to a contract to write scenarios for the movies. I don't think the children knew what a scenario was. I know I didn't.

I have always enjoyed movies and still do. Of course, I try to see only the good ones. It doesn't always turn out that way. I remember going to the movies and when they would roll the screen credits I would see Daniel Fuchs having written many Warner Bros. movies.

And then, many years later in 1956, he wrote the screenplay Love Me or Leave Me starring James Cagney and Doris Day and won the Oscar for Best Screenplay. I remember sitting in my apartment watching Mr. Fuchs accept the Academy Award.

In 1963 I moved to Los Angeles. In 1968, I happened to mention to another salesmen at Snyder and Son that my 4th grade teacher won an Academy Award. "He lives here and I would love to get in touch with him."

My co-worker suggested that I contact the Screen Writers' Guild. I took his advice, but was told that they were not allowed to give out phone numbers of any of their writers. I pleaded with the young lady, explaining that I was a tourist just passing through and that Daniel Fuchs was a teacher I had back in the fourth grade and that I may never get an opportunity to do this again. (Okay, so I fibbed.)

Guess what? She gave me his number. I called from the store and he answered the phone. I told him he had been my teacher in the fourth grade and that I had followed his career all these years, and that I was even watching TV when he received the Academy Award. He then asked my age. "Forty-seven," I replied. "Can you come over now?" "No," I replied, "but tomorrow is my day off." "Good," he said, "come tomorrow about 3 P.M. and we'll have coffee."

He had a lovely home on Bedford Drive in Beverly Hills and we had a nice visit but it was a little weird. I felt like I was 10-years-old again instead of 50. For example, I wanted to hold his Oscar, which he said was fine. I held it and imagined I was giving my acceptance speech, ignoring that they don't give Oscars for selling clothes. The Oscar was impressive, however and surprisingly heavy.) I carefully put it back on the mantle.

Then his wife came home and I recognized her, too as she had been a teacher at P.S. 225 before they married and left for Hollywood.

I'm a little embarrassed to admit I was struck by how old Mr. Fuchs appeared as I remembered him as my 23-year-old teacher. He was now in his seventies. (Or put another way, twenty years younger than I am now! Go figure.)

CHAPTER 55

NOT ENOUGH TIME WITH ARTIE (1974)

I wrote earlier how my father passed away when I was 12 and how that loss colored the rest of my life. Arthur passed almost exactly 40 years later. Dad was 42 when he passed, Artie was 47. As I told the checkout girl at Trader Joe's today, "My motto is, at 98, every day above the ground, is gravy."

I think about Artie and miss him very much every day. On reflection, we couldn't and didn't spend enough time together. This was partially because of the Great Depression during which I was always working after school. And then, when I was 19, we had Pearl Harbor—December 7th, 1941 and I started working in a defense plant twelve days later.

I worked 50 hours a week, 6 days a week, and saw very little of Artie. He was only 14 and in junior high school. Then in the spring of 1943, I left for Pearl Harbor to work at the Ford Island Naval Air Station and was 6,000 miles from Artie. However, he was always on my mind.

Artie was very mature for his age and also very intelligent. He teamed up with another kid his age and they put together a comedy act, calling themselves "The Star Gazers."

In those days, the comedians did impersonations. Mom told me that Artie did a great Groucho Marx. She actually saw him perform at the Audubon theater in the Bronx. I remember Artie writing me about a nightclub in Bridgeport, Connecticut, called "The Swiss Village," where he and his partner performed.

I also remember him writing that his partner didn't show up one night and Artie had to wing it all by himself. Having lied about his age just to get the booking, suddenly performing alone must have been very stressful for a 16-year-old.

Later when I came home from Hawaii in 1945, Artie was already in the Navy, stationed in Sampson, New York. When he was discharged in 1945, he got a job working as a recording technician. The hours were from 4 to midnight. Again, we hardly saw each other.

Also, the business he was in required that he work long hours. Through his wife Ronnie's wide acquaintanceship, her friends became his friends. In the meantime, the years flew by. His children, Mark and Heidi also kept him very busy.

When Artie passed, I realized that in the back of my mind I had hoped when I moved with Mom to L.A., that maybe he would follow me. I would have loved that. But it wasn't in the cards. I also realized with Artie gone, I was totally responsible for Mom's well being so I devoted much of my life to that. I suppose it's not done that way much these days but it was how I was brought up.

Artie & His Family, 1963

As for Artie, I think about him every day. In the meantime, I have my nieces and nephews, great nieces and nephews, a great, great niece and a great, great nephew due to arrive in August, all of whom keep me closely connected to Artie. And who knows, maybe someday he and I will be reunited.

ADDITIONAL PHOTOGRAPHS

Me at 18 months (Chapter 2)

Me at 1140 months

Honorable Discharge from The United States Army

TO ALL WHOM IT MAY CONCERN:

This is to Certify, That* *Morris Rosenblum*,
† *6430712* *Private* *602nd Ambulance Co.*

THE UNITED STATES ARMY, as a TESTIMONIAL OF HONEST AND FAITHFUL

SERVICE, is hereby HONORABLY DISCHARGED *from the military service of the*

UNITED STATES *by reason of* ‡ *Circular 106 W.D. 1918*

Said *Morris Rosenblum was born*

in *New York*, in the State of *New York*

When enlisted he was *27* years of age and by occupation a *Chauffeur*

He had *Gray* eyes, *Lt. Brown* hair, *Fair* complexion, and

was *5* feet *4 3/4* inches in height.

Given under my hand at *Camp Dix N.J.* this

26th day of *July*, one thousand nine hundred and *nineteen*

Johnson

Major U.S.A.

Commanding.

FORM No. 525, A. G. O.   *Insert name, Christian name first; e. g., "John Doe."
Oct. 9-18.   †Insert Army serial number, grade, company and regiment or arm or corps or department; e. g., "1,620,302"; "Corporal,
Company A, 1st Infantry"; "Sergeant, Quartermaster Corps"; "Sergeant, First Class, Medical Department."
2—3104   ‡ If discharged prior to expiration of service, give number, date, and source of order or full description of authority therefor.

Dad's WWI Honorable Discharge (Chapter 6)

Dad, cousin Herbert, uncle Jake, 1920

Me and Artie, 1929

Mom, me and Artie, Brighton Beach,1932

My buddies, "the 12th Street Boys."

Manny, Avey & Me, Pearl Harbor 1943 (Chapter 22)

Artie (Chapter 55)

Avey and Phoebe before tragedy struck, 1944 (Chapter 24)

Mom & me sunning in Santa Monica, 1983.

Esther Williams' 80th birthday party. (Chapter 76)

Watch out, Serena, cousin Jojo is coming. (Chapter 86)

Celebrating my being 1152 months.

Much appreciated birthday cards from Instagram friends.

My first podcast!

My great-great niece, Ella, who's beyond great.

WE NEED GUN CONTROL NOW

Thoughts and prayers aren't enough!

Katie's wonder dog, Teddy.

The girls took me out to the ball game.

I turned 1164 months.

My 2018 vacation and "D.A." Doug.

July 8, 2015

Mr. Jerry Rosenblum
1530 Fifth Street
Apartment 616
Santa Monica, CA 90401

Dear Mr. Rosenblum:

I heard the wonderful song and saw the delightful video you recorded for me and my campaign; thank you so much! I absolutely loved it, and I am so grateful for your enthusiasm and support.

I'm running for president to be a champion for everyday Americans and to forge a future where we don't leave anyone out or anyone behind. I know it won't be easy, and that there will be difficult days ahead, but I also know that I'm not alone. Thanks to your support, we're building a nationwide, grassroots effort that will inspire volunteers, mobilize voters, and carry us to victory.

Please know that I am sending you my best wishes for continued health and happiness. Onward!

With deep appreciation and warm regards, I am

Sincerely yours,

Hillary Rodham Clinton

Post Office Box 5256, New York, NY 10185 · www.hillaryclinton.com
Contributions or gifts to Hillary for America are not tax deductible.

Paid for by Hillary for America

Thank you from HRC (Chapter 94)

Jerry and Sheila.

Congresswoman Alexandria Ocasio-Cortez and Jerry 12/21/2019
(Photos courtesy Sheila Laffey)

My message of hope to all.

CHAPTER 56

AFTER SIX SHOWS IN A ROW, I WAS ALL "MERVED" OUT (1975)

In his early days, Merv Griffin was a singer who also played piano in the Freddie Martin Orchestra. The band played one weekend at a beach club that I got to attend. (Albeit because Marty and I sneaked in!) I remember Merv singing, "I've Got A Lovely Bunch of Coconuts," which turned out to be a huge hit and sold millions of records.

Years later, I was a big fan of the "Merv Griffin Show." I liked his easy going personality and humor and the interesting guests who would appear. I always wanted to attend but I was too busy with work.

In the early 70s, Merv moved his show to LA. and, amazingly, I got my chance. By then, I was managing Snyder & Son at the Century Plaza Hotel. One afternoon, Arthur Treacher, Merv sidekick on the show, walked in. I recognized him immediately and explained I was one of Merv most loyal fans. I know it took chutzpah, but I even mentioned I always wanted to see his show in person.

"That can be arranged, Sir," he replied, "How many in your party?" I looked around the store and came up with the number six. He said, "Tomorrow around 12:30 P.M. Mr. Griffin's secretary will hand deliver your tickets." I thanked him profusely, then he bought some clothes and left.

The next day, as promised, a very attractive young lady handed me an envelope containing six tickets to the "Merv Griffin Show." Griffin was doing his show relatively nearby at CBS Studios on Fairfax and Beverly Blvd.

When we arrived at the studio, people were standing in a long line but our tickets were VIP and we were ushered right in and seated in the second row orchestra. We saw a great show that included Steve Allen and Liberace. Everyone in the group thanked me for arranging the tickets.

Little did I know, that Treacher had arranged for VIP tickets for us on a daily basis. Every afternoon, around the same time, Merv's secretary would hand me an envelope with six tickets inside. It was great. For a while.

We continued going to the shows until we all got kinda tired of the routine. I'm reminded of the expression, "too much of a good thing." Diplomatically, as I could, I called Merv's office, "Listen, I really appreciated all the tickets but, at least for now, we need to take a break." Merv was great, but enough was enough.

I still continued to watch Merv on TV. I also enjoyed the great success he achieved with his game shows and hotels, which made him a billionaire! And to think it all started with a lovely bunch of coconuts.

CHAPTER 57

COMEDIAN FLIP WILSON GOT THE LAST LAUGH (1975)

This chapter involves the late and renowned African-American comedian, Flip Wilson, host of a hit weekly television show on NBC. He was young, handsome, intelligent, and quick on his feet. He was also becoming a very big star.

Every week a man connected with the show would come into our store in the Century Plaza Hotel to select what Flip would wear on his upcoming show. Snyder & Son, would get credit for Flip's wardrobe when they rolled the screen credits. It would read: "Flip Wilson's Wardrobe by Snyder & Son, Century Plaza Hotel, Century City, Los Angeles."

Well, this went on for months until finally I told his wardrobe manager that it would be nice if Flip would pay us a visit. Sure enough, the following day Flip showed up.

In the east back then, many men were wearing fur coats. I had made a deal with Dicker and Dicker, a store in the hotel that sold fur coats to let us put a couple of their fur coats on our selling floor. And if one or more sold we would figure out our commission.

As soon as Flip entered the store he saw the fur coat and immediately asked to try it on. It fit him perfectly and he was enthralled. However, when he was admiring himself in the mirror he noticed our cashier, Bonnie, who was on the buxom side and happened to be showing lots of cleavage. Flip took off the coat and, without another word, walked over to her and begins to flirt.

Flirting back, Bonnie told Flip that she had a very jealous husband, so much so that when he goes out of town on a business trip, he makes her wear a chastity belt.

Flip, the comedian that he was, came right back with a remark that broke up everyone in the store. He told Bonnie that he wasn't always a comedian. She replied, "Oh, really and what exactly did you do for a living before you were a comedian?" Without missing a beat, Flip said, " I was a "locksmith."

CHAPTER 58

A DRUNK WITH A GUN, A SCARY COMBINATION (1975)

I moved to Santa Monica in 1971. It was a great move. Mom and I lived in an apartment building across the from Palisades Park and one of the world's great ocean views. It was also right across the street from a senior citizens' center. Mom would spend part of her day with new friends she met there. I was working and, on my days off, I would play shuffleboard on a court next to the senior center. I learned the game quickly and became quite a good player. Sundays were always the busiest on the shuffleboard courts.

One Sunday afternoon in July, I was playing and the courts were very busy. Every court was taken and spectators were sitting on a bench, watching the games. Suddenly, a man appeared, walking like he had too much to drink. It was pretty obvious that he was going to become a problem. He began using a lot of foul language and, of all things, he was wearing an overcoat in July. At that point, one of the seniors in our shuffleboard club said, "Jerry, can you do anything about this guy? He's ruining our game."

He came to me because, at 53, I was by far the youngest member in our club and in the best shape. (You know what they say, if you're overweight and want to look thinner, hang out with fat people. So in this group, I was a "youngster,")

I looked at this drunken, irrational-sounding nut-cake and thought to myself, "If I give him any lip, who knows what he's liable to do?" Then, just when we needed them, a police car came riding up close to the shuffleboard court and stopped.

Two cops came out of the car and walked over to the drunk and directed him to put both hands against a nearby tree. He complied and they started to frisk him. Try to imagine how I felt when one of the cops removed a revolver from one of his overcoat pockets.

They immediately slapped handcuffs on him, put him into the patrol car and left.

Who knows what could have happened had I gotten into an argument with him? It kinda put a chill on the shuffleboard game, if you follow my drift.

CHAPTER 59

BING CROSBY WAS GOING MY WAY
(1976)

In the store one morning I was on my knees as I adjusted ties in the semi-circular neck wear case we had close to the entrance. I was aware that a man had entered so I stood up and came face to face with Bing Crosby. "Hi, Bing," I blurted out like we had known each other our whole lives. It's kind of understandable in a weird way, because, in fact, Bing was born in 1903 and by the time I listened to records and radio, it seemed he was always on both.

"Hi," he said back with that soothing voice of his. "I need a pair of beige slacks." "I think we can manage that," I said, surprised by how relaxed Bing made me feel. After looking at the slim selection of slacks in his size 36 waist, I realized the only pants I had that would fit him in the color he wanted was in a style that was a little passé.

It had a flair bottom and, as such,was a bit dated. Bing didn't mind at all. "I'm going to use them for golf and I'll probably get mud all over the bottom of them, anyway. So, it's okay. I'll take them." While he was in the dressing room putting on the slacks, I was carrying on a conversation with him as I suppose I am wont to do. But he had started it from the dressing room so I just kept it going.

I had read a biography about him a couple of years before in which he described a party he had attended. The host was so wealthy he actually had a bowling alley in his home. I asked Bing if that really was true. "Oh, yes. It was true." I then asked him if he sees Bob Hope often, considering they made several movies together. "Yes," he said. "We got together occasionally."

Bing Crosby couldn't have been nicer. He was just a real mensch, or so he seemed. I say that because, only months later, I saw him on a Barbara Walters TV Special and I was stunned by something he said that I can never forget. Barbara was even more stunned, than I was.

Walters brought up the subject of his youngest daughter, Mary, who was a fledgling actress and also a fledgling hippy, free spirit. Barbara asked Bing if he would have a problem if Mary ever moved in with her boyfriend without the benefit of marriage.

Cold as ice, Bing responded, "No, I wouldn't have a problem, because she would no longer be my daughter." Barbara was shocked. "You can't be serious, Bing." "I'm very serious," he said casually and without any emotion. "Any daughter of mine would know that I would never condone such an immoral situation. So if she did it, it's quite simple, she would no longer be my daughter."

I thought Barbara was going to have a stroke. Ironically and sadly, less than a year later, Bing died in Madrid of a heart attack. His public persona had been that of such an easy going man, but in real life, it appears he was anything but. Especially when it came to his kids. I've come to accept that it's a mistake to judge what a person says on the outside,without knowing what they really think on the inside.

CHAPTER 60

MOM MURDERS 'EM AT THE GONG SHOW (1976)

In 1976, Mom and I were watching a new program on TV, "The Gong Show," which ran from 1976-1978. Employing "absurdest humor" For those not familiar, the show consisted of amateur (sometimes, painfully so) singers, dancers, musicians, and comedians, who would perform in front of three celebrity judges and a live audience.

The show had a four-piece orchestra and they accompanied the performers when necessary. The idea was to be able to get through the act without getting "gonged" on the big metal gong, and thus removed from the show, but all in good fun. You could say the show was so bad, it was good, if that makes any sense.

If the performer didn't get "gonged," the judges then gave him or her a score from 1 to 25. If a performer was good enough to receive a 25 from all three judges, in all likelihood, that person would receive the grand prize of a not so whopping five hundred dollars. The fun part was listening to the judges' comments after each act, especially if the act was gonged.

Well, the night we were watching it so happened a friend of Mom's (Helen Jacobson) sang a song and won the grand prize.(Which wasn't very grand.) I could see that Mom was furious. "She never mentioned a word about it," referring to Helen's secrecy.

"You've got to get me an audition for that show." At the end of each show they would tell viewers who wanted to audition to call the number on the screen. We made the call and a few days later drove to Hollywood for the audition.

They gave Mom an application to fill out, which I helped her with. Mom always made herself two years younger than she really was so instead of writing seventy-nine, she put seventy-seven.

Finally, it was her turn to audition in front of producer Chuck Barris. The song was "Never on Sunday" from the hit film, Never on Sunday. Barris liked her performance and said, "You're on the show next week." It happened just that fast! Mom was to report to the NBC studios in Burbank at 8 on Saturday morning. I was simultaneously thrilled and worried.

I brought her there on time and said I'd be back later in the afternoon as I had to work that day, but managed to get off early. I said to Mom that I hoped she wouldn't be nervous. "Why should I be nervous?" she replied. "I know what I'm going to do. Let them be nervous." That was classic mom.

Back in 1976, there were no VCR's, so after Mom and I saw the show when it aired, that was it. Over the years, Mom often said she'd love to be able to see herself again on The Gong Show. Finally, one day I decided to do something about it.

After making several phone calls, I finally found out who owned the tapes of The Gong Show, a company in West LA owned by Jon Peters and Peter Guber financed by the Sony Corp. They were in an office building on Bundy Drive near Olympic. a fifteen-minute drive from Santa Monica.

I made the call and asked to speak to Jon Peter's secretary. (Peters was Barbra Streisand's boyfriend at the time.) The young lady couldn't have been nicer. I explained why I was calling. She told me the tapes were in a warehouse in the Valley. She would dispatch one of her assistants to look for the tape in which Mom appeared.

Not only did they find the tape, but made four copies, one for my sister-in-law, one for my niece, one for my nephew and one for us. Securing that tape was one of the best moves I ever made.

The show Mom was on was one of the best shows of The Gong Show series. It was repeated and Mom received residuals of about three hundred dollars. When she began singing, "You Can Kiss Me on a Monday," each judge got out of his chair, walked over to Mom while she was still singing and gave her a kiss. The judges were Milton Berle, Soupy Sales, and Ruth Buzzi, and they kissed her in that order. I've played that tape many times and I get such a kick out of seeing Mom and remember the events that led up to that show.

Remember that Milton Berle was one of the judges? I say that because Mom ran into him years later and, suffice it to say, Uncle Milty wasn't exactly thrilled. That story is coming soon, so stay tuned!

CHAPTER 61

ONE DEGREE OF SEPARATION FROM THE HILLSIDE STRANGLERS (1976)

In 1976, there used to be a bakery on Rose Avenue near Main Street in Venice that sold day-old bread at very reduced prices and yet it was still delicious. Mom told me that we could use some bread and were close by, so I parked in front of the place and Mom went in to buy bread. I sat in the car and waited.

I inadvertently looked out onto the road and noticed an old wallet lying in the street. I picked it up and brought it into the car. There wasn't any money but there was a driver's license and some business cards. The wallet belonged to a very pretty 19-year-old girl named Cindy Hudspeth. That name would come to haunt me as you'll see.

When I came back to the apartment, I looked in the phone book and found Cindy's phone number. Her name also appeared on a business card I found in her wallet. The card was for a modeling agency. I called and told her I found her wallet and gave her my address. I told her she could come and get her things.

She lived in Malibu, which wasn't too far away. In about an hour she showed up and rang my bell. I handed her the wallet and she was very appreciative. She was a thin, young girl and, sadly, unusually pretty as she was, she nonetheless looked like a lost soul. Somehow. I wanted to say something or ask if she wanted to talk, but she would have thought I was weird.

I can't explain it, I just had a bad feeling about her and felt helpless to do anything. As she kissed me on the cheek, I could only hope I was wrong.

Her last name was unusual—Hudspeth. I had never before come across that name and somehow it stayed in my memory. A few months later, newspapers and TV in

Los Angeles were broadcasting and writing constantly about two alleged murderers referred to as the "Hillside Stranglers"—Kenneth Bianchi and his cousin, Angelo Buono. These two were picking up girls in their car, raping them, and then strangling them. They would toss the girls' bodies out of their vehicle into the remote hillside.

These psychopathic monsters were finally arrested and convicted of murdering 10 women ages, 12-28. In 1983, both received life sentences without the possibility of parole. In 2002, Buono died of natural causes. Bianchi, who was married in 1989, will spend the rest of his life in a Washington State Prison.

After their arrest, a list of Hillside Strangler victims appeared in the Los Angeles Times. A chill went up and down my spine as I read the article. Shockingly, Bianchi and Buono's last victim was... Cindy Hudspeth.

Cindy was someone's daughter and grand daughter, someone's sister and niece now her life was senselessly over at 19. She was such a pretty, young girl whom I felt needed help, maybe even someone to talk to. I would have gladly listened but it was not to be.

As I put down the paper, I was overcome with sadness.

CHAPTER 62

OLD BLUE EYES WAS NOT FOND OF MOTOR MOUTH (1977)

This chapter took place in 1977. While working at Snyder & Son at the Century Plaza Hotel, I had made friends with the hotel's veteran house detective. One Saturday morning he came into the store to tell me that I should call my mother, whom he knew was a big fan of many celebrities. He confided that at about 1 p.m. Frank Sinatra, one of Mom's favorite performers, was going to come to the hotel to rehearse his act.

The performance was to be a benefit concert for Jim Stacey, a very popular and talented actor, who was married to actress Connie Stevens, as it happens. Recently, Stacey had suffered a terrible motorcycle accident, causing him to lose an arm and a leg.

The biggest stars in show business rallied to his support and decided to give him a benefit in the hotel's Grand Ballroom. Mom was to arrive just at the time when the rehearsals would start. The detective would bring her down to the ballroom and personally seat her in the first row. The biggest names in show business would be rehearsing.

Frank Sinatra, who had been retired, decided to make a comeback and this benefit was to be his reemergence as a top entertainer. Sammy Davis, Jr. would be there, as well as Liza Minnelli, the Pointer Sisters, and many more. If one were to go to Las Vegas and pay to see all this entertainment, sitting in the first row, it could cost thousands of dollars.

So, Mom arrived on time, however, she brought her friend, Hilda Katz, who, unfortunately, gave new meaning to the term "motor mouth." Though I tried to be patient with her, Hilda couldn't stop talking. Ever. It was a nervousness she had and it couldn't be controlled. Hilda was exactly the wrong person to bring to a rehearsal of this kind. The first performer to rehearse was Sammy Davis, Jr. Next was Liza Minnelli.

I remember coming down to the Grand Ballroom to see how Mom was doing. Well, I could see Mom and Hilda were having a great time, so I went back up to the store where I was needed. While in the ballroom, I noticed Sinatra, who sat with friends and was due to rehearse next. We made eye contact and that was all.

About a half hour later, Mom and Hilda Katz come walking into the store. I wasn't expecting them so soon and asked what happened. Mom told me the security guard asked them to leave. It seems Hilda was annoying Sinatra with her constant chattering. This benefit was very important to Sinatra because of all the important people who would be attending. He was being very fussy with musicians, making sure they played the arrangements to his liking.

The "Chairman of the Board" had quite a temper

Sinatra was highly annoyed by "motor mouth." He called over one of the guards and said, "Get rid of those two broads." Ouch. Given it was Hilda, I couldn't blame him.

CHAPTER 63

JESSE OWENS WAS AS NICE AS HE WAS GIFTED (1978)

In the 1970's there was a short-lived fashion fad in men's clothing that might seem very strange today. Actually, it seemed a little strange at the time. I'm referring to men wearing leisure suits. Extremely convenient, it was a one piece garment that men slipped into, zipped up and tied at the waist.

These leisure suits were usually made from a polyester fabric but they also came in corduroy. I remember we had one on display in our show window. While they weren't my taste at all, for a while the item was so popular we tried to keep a full range of sizes.

Well, one day an African-American couple, guests of the hotel, came into the store. They were seniors and the gentleman asked to try on the leisure suit on display. We didn't have one in his size but I explained that I could order one in his size, alter it and send it to him.

He agreed and gave me his name and address. As he did, I almost stopped dead in my tracks. It turned out I had been waiting on one of the most famous athletes of all time—the legendary Jesse Owens.

Jesse won 4 Gold Medals, Adolf got heartburn.

In 1936, Jesse Owens won four Olympic gold medals at the games held in Berlin, Germany. I remember as a kid going to the movies and watching him in the newsreels. I remember how angry Adolph Hitler was when Jesse came in first, ahead of the star German competitor. Hitler was visibly furious and showed how prejudiced he was.

I remember Mr. Owens offered to pay for the suit in advance. I said that wouldn't be necessary because I wasn't sure whether the manufacturer had it in stock. I would know on Monday when they reopened. I told him if the factory had one in his size I would send it to him, I would enclose a bill and then he could mail us a check. I remember the sale amount amounted to $100 and that he lived in Phoenix, Arizona.

I ordered the leisure suit for him. They had it in stock and I shipped it as promised. Mr. Owens sent a check and I never saw him again. I've waited on so many famous customers in my fifty years as a clothing salesman, but this particular sale stands out in my memory because, in addition to being such an extraordinary athlete, Jesse was such an extraordinary gentleman.

It's possible you might have had to live through the rise of fascism in Europe in the 1930's to understand what Jesse accomplished at the '36 Olympics. Hitler and his demented Nazi followers, wanted to show the world the superiority of the white race. When Jesse, an African-American, won those 4 Gold Medals, in it's own way, it proved the fallacy of Hitler's thinking and was a triumph for democracy. (With democracy declining all over the world in favor of authoritarianism, we could use Jesse today.)

CHAPTER 64

"UNCLE MILTY" COULD ALSO BE "UNCLE MEANIE" (1978)

It was very exciting working at the shop at the Century Plaza. You never knew who would walk into the store. One day in came Milton Berle, who was the very first TV star with his famous Texaco Star Theater program, which ran from 1948 to 1956. Because of the enormous success of the show, Berle became known as "Mr. Television."

So it was Mr. Television, also known as "Uncle Milty," asked if I had a black mohair suit in a size 43 long. I had exactly what he asked for and after he tried on the jacket he agreed to take it. I then escorted him to the dressing room so he could try on the pants.

While this was going on, Bill Snyder, one of the owners, was having a phone conversation on the other side of the store. He finally got through talking and came over to where I was waiting for Mr. Berle to come out of the dressing room. Berle came out just at the same time that Billy came to my side. Berle was ready to be fitted and Billy said to him, "Oh, hello, Mr. Schwartz."

Mortally wounded that someone had the "audacity" to not recognize him, Berle looked at me and said, "Who the hell is that?" Billy then realized his faux pas. "Please excuse me, Mr. Berle. I didn't recognize you. I don't have my glasses on." "Yeah, well you better put them on," Berle replied. "Apparently you really need them."

Believe it or not, there's considerably more to Uncle Milty, involving of all people, my mother. My mother spent a lot of time at the Israel Levin Center for seniors on the border of Santa Monica and Venice. It is a wonderful organization and provides such a great service to our seniors, including my Mom, the memories of which still brings joy to my heart.

Often the Center would get free tickets for plays, concerts and other show business events. This time they were invited to attend a Friar's Club meeting. The Friar's is a world famous group of almost primarily comedians who get together for laughs but also they do great philanthropic work. So my mother was thrilled to attend.

Once there, my mother recognized Milton Berle on the dais. You'll recall that my mother was once a contestant on "The Gong Show" and one of the judges was Uncle Milty.

Here's where it gets a little nuanced. No offense, but to be a judge on "The Gong Show" was not necessarily a good sign about your career. It reminds me of the "Celebrity Apprentice." If you were on that show, guess what? You're not really a celebrity anymore. But my mother couldn't help herself, she had to remind Berle of their "past."

Uncle Milty, wasn't exactly thrilled. As my mother kept rambling on and fairly loudly so others might have been able to overhear, he gave her a "shush" sign and said, "Lady, let's keep this between us, okay?"

My mother said okay but she really didn't understand all the fuss. She was a pistol and I miss her dearly.

CHAPTER 65

THE CRIMINAL RETURNS TO THE SCENE OF THE CRIME (1979)

Here's another true story about what can happen in the retail business. It took place on a normal Saturday afternoon. A fellow came into the store carrying lots of bags, obviously from other stores, indicating he had done a fair amount of shopping. There were so many he could hardly manage them all.

Allan, one of the salesmen, sold him a $295 leather jacket. The transaction was handled through American Express. We received the approval for the charge and gave him the jacket in a garment bag, so he added one more package to the load he was carrying. He had been a busy boy that afternoon, though at that moment I had no idea as to what kind of "busy" he had been.

About ten minutes after he left, the store received a call from American Express. "Is that customer still in the store?" they asked. "No," the cashier replied. The voice on the other end explained that the guy who gave us the American Express card had used a stolen card. Because we had called it in and received the approval, we were off the hook and American Express would have to cover the charge.

Allan said he would go to lunch and maybe he would see the thief in the Century City Shopping Center. He came back after lunch and reported the he was nowhere to be found. An hour later, about 2:30 P.M., I saw the same guy with all of his various packages, including ours, looking in a jewelry shop window next to our store.

I whispered to Billy Snyder, "Look who came back to the scene of the crime." When Billy saw who it was he couldn't believe the idiot would actually come back to the hotel. Just then, I got an idea. "Hey, fella!" I called out to him. "You left one of your packages here when you bought the jacket." He fell for the bait and came in, packages and all.

Billy was seventy-eight years old at the time. I was in my late 50's. Ray Marshall, however, was seventeen years younger than me. As soon as the jerk stepped into the store, Billy, despite his senior citizen status, went up behind him and put both arms around him in a very tight grip. This caused the crook to drop all the parcels.

He then broke loose from Billy and started running from the store through the corridor leading to the main lobby. Well, Ray was right behind him and I was just behind Ray. Just by luck, Ray caught up to him, tackled him and brought him down. At that exact moment, the house detective, a retired professional football player who stood 6'4" and weighed 220, arrived on the scene—just when we needed him.

He put handcuffs on the thief and brought him back to the store and held him in the back room. The police were notified and took him away with all the evidence. I think American Express gave the store a reward for the capture and subsequent confiscation of the card.

Billy was proud of his exploits that afternoon. However, as he felt sore later in the day, he lamented, "Actually, I think I'm getting too old for this." Ah, the retail business. After experiences like this, you learn to appreciate the dull moments.

CHAPTER 66

THEY CALLED HIM MR. TIBBS (1962, 1979 & 2009)

One day in 1962, while I was working at Kallen's, Sidney Poitier walked into the store. I recognized him immediately. Unfortunately, Benny Levine was up on call and he was the lucky one to sell Poitier a navy blue suit. He was rather tall (6'2") and Benny sold him a 40 extra long, navy blue suit. (I know it's odd that I not only remember running into these people but I remember what they bought.)

After Sidney left, I told Benny that he had just waited on a major movie star. (Poitier had starred in Porgy and Bess in 1959). But Benny didn't know the difference between Sidney Poitier and Sydney Greenstreet.

In 1964, Poitier became the first African-American to win a Best Actor Academy Award with his role in Lilies of the Field. And who can forget his performances in Guess Who's Coming to Dinner? and In the Heat of the Night, which, for me, is a near perfect movie. (As I edit this in 2019, I saw it not long ago and it's remarkable how well it holds up.)

Cut to 1979 and I had long ago relocated to Los Angeles. It was a Sunday afternoon at about 4:00 P.M. I had closed the store and was coming out of the back entrance of the Century Plaza. I was carrying the "Calendar" section of the Los Angeles Times, which featured Sidney Poitier's picture on the front page.

In going to my car, I had to pass Yamato's Japanese Restaurant. Just then, a car pulled up in front of the restaurant and out stepped Poitier. As he passed in front of me, I held out the "Calendar" Section and smiled. He smiled back so appreciatively I felt a kinship. I was thrilled, after all, what are the odds that holding the Calendar Section I'd run into the subject of the Calendar Section.

Now we cut to the Beverly Hills Civic Center in 2011. Poitier was there to introduce someone he admires enormously, Angella Nazarian an Iranian-Jewish immigrant and famed non-fiction author. Her first book, Life as a Visitor, chronicled her departure from Iran and life as a refugee in California. Her second, Pioneers of the Possible: Celebrating Visionary Women of the World, is a collection of essays about female role models. Her third book, Visionary Women, highlights the lives of twenty female luminaries of modern times.

I arrived typically early and spotted Poitier. I asked his assistant if I might talk to him briefly and Mr. Poitier was very gracious in inviting me over. (Out of my enormous respect for him, I referred to him as "Mr. Poitier" throughout our brief conversation.) I related that I first saw him in person in 1962 and that he purchased a navy blue suit that was a 40 extra long. He got a real kick out of that, acknowledging he had gained weight over the years and his 40 extra long days were "extra long gone."

I briefly mentioned "In the Heat of the Night" and told him that Stirling Silliphant, the screenwriter and Rod Steiger, the actor, both of whom won Oscars for that movie, were also customers of mine as was Carroll O'Connor who played Sheriff Gillespie for the 8 years of the TV show. He seemed intrigued with all these "coincidences."

My last "offering" was when I showed Mr. Poitier a photo of himself in Venice, Italy, standing next to my great-nephew. The photo was taken by his mother Heidi, whose wall at home is filled with her standing next to famous celebrities. Mr. Poitier smiled, "So this 'trait' runs in your family?" "Apparently," I said, as we both laughed.

CHAPTER 67

LIFE IS BUT A CIRCLE (1978)

Now here's a very unusual story, although given my life experience, I suppose it's not that unusual. At the time this story began it was 1950 and the population of the U.S. was 150,000,000.

Back then, Mom and I lived on East 9th Street. In truth, we longed for an apartment in Brighton Beach but they were incredibly difficult to find. Not surprisingly, lots of people wanted to live as close to the beach as possible.

Living in Brighton Beach in the summer would have been very desirable. It was much cooler than the city and closer to the Beach Club, a blue collar club where we had lockers. The superintendents of the various buildings in Brighton all had long waiting lists of people who wanted to move in when an apartment became available. I'm sure prospective tenants were bribing the supers to move their names up on the list.

About this time I was reading the classified section and an ad caught my eye that for five hundred dollars a Brighton Beach apartment was available, furniture and all. The apartment had a living room, bedroom and kitchen. I rushed over to check it out.

It seemed perfect and I loved the location on Brighton 6th Street near Brighton Beach Avenue. As I showed the man five one-hundred-dollar bills, I asked, "What about the super?"

He explained he had made a deal directly with the landlord. They would split the five hundred dollars between them. So I immediately went to see the landlord. He confirmed everything so I took the deal with great delight. Mom and I happily spent the next thirteen years of our life there.

Now, fast forward to 1980 where we first started this story. I had been working in the hotel shop of the Century Plaza Hotel for twelve years. I was crossing the lobby one lunchtime on the way to the employee cafeteria. I happened to look out toward the beautiful Japanese gardens and saw Jackie Cooper, the actor and director, being interviewed about the upcoming fall television shows. I stopped to listen to the interview. An elderly couple was standing next to me.

"Is that Jackie Cooper?" the man asked. "Yes," I replied. "My God," he said, "I feel so old! I remember when Jackie was a child actor," He was speaking a little too loudly so, rather than disturb the interview, I suggested all three of us go back into the lobby where we could continue our discussion.

"Where are you from?" he asked. I told him, "I'm the manager of the clothing store," and I pointed in that direction. "No," he said. "I mean, where are you from originally?" "New York," I replied. "I thought so. That's where we're from," he said. "But now we live in Florida. We're here visiting our daughter. Where did you live in New York?"

When I said Brighton Beach, he exclaimed, "Brighton Beach?!" We lived there, too. Where in Brighton?" I told him 3085 Brighton at 6th Street. "That's unbelievable," he exclaimed. "We lived at 3085 Brighton at 6th Street, too!" (Are you sensing where this is going?)

Now we began to look at each other more closely. "What apartment did you live in?" he asked. "Apartment C-12, I replied." "Wait a minute. We lived in Apartment C-12, too!" he exclaimed. It was only then that we both figured it out. This was the man I had given five hundred dollars to in order to buy the option to rent his apartment thirty years ago.

I'm not sure what it says about me, that these sorts of "coincidences" or whatever they are, happen so often. I'm grateful that they have if, for no other reason, than they make up a great deal of this book! But then again, if you've gotten this far, you probably know that already.

CHAPTER 68

J.F.K. GAVE SOME GOOD ADVICE (1979)

Red Boucher was the Lieutenant Governor of Alaska but he would often visit friends in Los Angeles. And when he did, he stayed at the Century Plaza Hotel and would shop at Snyder & Son. A salesman named Ray would always take care of Lt. Governor Boucher when he came in. However, one Sunday, Lt. Governor Boucher came in when it was Ray's day off. I knew the Lt. Governor from his previous visits.

He insisted I call him Red, instead of Lt. Governor. That was fine by me as saying Lt. Governor over and over was a bit cumbersome. Red had a specific item of clothing in mind. He asked if I had a sport coat that had the colors red, white and blue in it.

Evidently he was due to make a speech in Alaska on July the 4th and wanted to wear these colors. Odd as it may sound, a couple of days before we received a shipment of sports jackets from a top manufacturer. These jackets had red, white and blue in the fabric. The coat was made in Switzerland and very fine 100% polyester. As soon as he tried it on, Red realized that it was exactly what he was looking for and was very pleased.

By the time the fitter had tailored the jacket and the transaction was completed, it was 3:30 P.M. I looked out into the lobby and didn't see a soul. I needed to kill another half an hour until closing. "Red," I said, "if you're in no hurry to leave, let me pour you a glass of sherry and we can chat for half an hour."

Red happily agreed and we began to talk and I discovered he was exactly 1 year older than I was. I soon asked him how he got into politics. Mind you, this is the Lieutenant Governor of Alaska. But I have a feeling the conversation, and maybe more likely the sherry, loosened his tongue a bit.

He explained that he was in the Navy during World War II and served on the USS PT 109, one of the hundreds of motor torpedo boats commissioned by the United States Navy. It also happened to be the PT boat that Lieutenant John F. Kennedy commanded.

During one of their many conversations, Kennedy asked Red, a fellow Irishman who was born and raised in New Hampshire, what he intended to do when the war ended. "I'm saving my money to buy a gas station." Red answered.

JFK's eyes lit up. He told Red that, with his savings, Red should consider going to Alaska because eventually it was going to be declared a state. He also suggested that when Red moved there he should join service organizations. "Try to become popular and well-liked. Before you know it you may want to run for public office."

Red took Kennedy's advice and it definitely worked. He was once Mayor of Fairbanks, served 3 terms in the Alaska House of Representatives and finally worked his way up to within a heartbeat of the governorship of Alaska.

Interestingly, Red was also the founder of the Alaska Goldpanners, a minor league baseball team whose alumni included: Barry Bonds, Tom Seaver, Terry Francona, Jason Giambi, Bob Boone, Andy Messersmith, Dave Kingman, Dave Winfield, Graig Nettles and Rick Monday. Some list! Red was instrumental in the formation of the Alaska Baseball League and was the Goldpanners' manager for ten seasons, posted a 337-118 record and was admitted into the Alaska Sports Hall of Fame. Wow! (Fortunately I had the good sense not to discuss my stick ball exploits in Brooklyn.)

Once again, here I am, shooting the breeze with the Lieutenant Governor of Alaska, as if we were old buddies. All I can say, as with so many people I've written about in this memoir, it certainly felt like it. Go figure.

CHAPTER 69

THE HIGH CLASS HOOKER & THE LEATHER JACKET (1979)

I've learned the hard way that when you're in retail sales, and I'm sure, lots of other businesses, you can be sure there will be someone trying to put one over on you. This incident took place at the hotel shop on a Saturday afternoon about 5:00 P.M.—closing time was at 6:00 P.M. A young man came into the store with an attractive, middle-aged woman he told us was his "aunt" who wanted to buy him a fancy leather jacket.

I found a jacket that fit him well. The jacket was imported from Spain and in those days it sold for $295. Today, the jacket would be priced at about $650. I wrote out a sales slip and asked how she wanted to pay for it. "I'll give you my check," she replied. "Do you have a credit card?" I asked. "No," she replied, "My check is good and there is nothing to worry about."

I explained that in this situation, I couldn't release the merchandise until the check cleared. I told her, "You see company policy, for a first-time customer intending to take the merchandise with them, is that the merchandise has to remain in the store until the bank opens and we can verify the check." She looked legitimate but something didn't "smell right." I just couldn't bring myself to okay the check. Thankfully.

Billy Snyder, the store owner's father, was in the back office. He was Bob's father and had considerably more experience dealing with people than I had. I excused myself for a minute and went back to speak to Billy. After I explained the circumstances, Billy peeked out to get a look at the couple in question.

"They look okay," he said. "If you say so, Billy," I replied. "Then in that case how about you okaying the check?" He did. To protect the store as much as possible I took the young man's identification and home address and the woman's address and iden-tification. We completed the sale and I gave them the jacket. Guess what? A few days later, the check came back stamped "NSF." Billy Snyder was furious. How could he have been so naive?

That night, after we closed the store, we headed to Burton Way in Beverly Hills where the alleged "aunt" had an apartment in a security building. The garage entrance was gated but just then an automobile was leaving. When the gate went up we ran into the garage.

We rode up to the "aunt's" floor, found her apartment, rang the doorbell and knocked several times. It was very quiet; no one appeared to be home. We struck out on that one.

We then headed for Beverly Glen, just south of Wilshire, where the young man lived. He was home and very surprised to see us. We were glad to see him because now we could retrieve the jacket. He gave the jacket back to us very reluctantly, claiming he hadn't had a chance to wear it.

"Good," I said. I demanded he tell me who the woman was and if she really was his aunt. He then confessed because I had also told him we could have him arrested. He proceeded to tell us the whole story. He said he was going to UCLA and working after school as a waiter in a very posh, exclusive men's club that had mostly multimil-lionaires as members.

It seems the woman, posing as his aunt, was actually a high-priced prostitute. He was acting as her pimp. After several successful liaisons, they decided the jacket was to be his payoff. The woman really lived in Long Beach but kept the Burton Way apartment because it was minutes from her "potential clients" at the exclusive men's club.

We were happy to get the jacket back and called it a day. A very unusual, very weird, and long day at that.

CHAPTER 70

A MIDDLE EAST CRISIS IN CENTURY CITY (1970 & 1980)

I have made lists of all the notable people I have waited on. The list includes Abba Eban, the former Israeli Foreign Minister. I took care of him twice, with a ten-year interval. The first time was in 1970. Mr. Eban was at the Century Plaza to address the United Jewish Appeal and raise money for worthy causes. Unfortunately, the Arab League was very militant at that time. As a result when the news leaked out that Abba Eban was staying at the hotel, there were big demonstrations in front of the hotel.

The picketers were very vocal and the police had their hands full. Making matters more tense, the Jewish Defense League was there, too, with their signs. At the height of all the excitement, Abba Eban walked into the store with three Secret Service Men—one on either side of him with their hands in their inside jacket pockets, I assumed holding guns. A third agent stationed himself at the entrance of the store, also with a gun, and he was talking to someone on a walkie-talkie. This was before cell phones.

Somewhat urgently, Eban spoke to me. "My wife forgot to pack my formal bow tie," said Eban. I found a tie to his liking and asked how long he intended to stay at the hotel. We were standing next to the showcase that stocked sport shirts. I said to him, "If you have three minutes to spare, I'd like to show you sport shirts you may want to wear while you're in LA." I suggested two shirts, in particular, and he bought both.

I felt honored that it was my good fortune to take care of such a distinguished gentleman. He thanked me, paid his bill and left to get into his tuxedo. As I said, this took place 1970.

In 1980, Abba Eban checked into the Century Plaza Hotel a second time. He was no longer the Israeli Foreign Minister but still a highly regarded world figure. Again, I waited on him and diplomatically reminded him about the demonstrations, the yelling and the shouting ten years earlier. He remembered them and even remembered me.

As it happens, also in 1980, the US was honoring a treaty with Panama. We had agreed to turn over the Panama Canal to Panama. Carter was President and he was determined to honor our commitments. I asked Mr. Eban if he thought the U.S. was doing the right thing. He agreed that we were. Maybe it's just me, but I found it fascinating to listen to a former world leader opine on the current political events of the day.

CHAPTER 71

WHEN THE GOING GETS TOUGH, HIT THE ROLODEX (1978)

Of all the jobs I had in my working career, the twelve years that I worked for Snyder & Son were the most enjoyable. The store had been there right from the opening day of the Century Plaza Hotel. The hotel opened for business in 1963. I began working there on November 6th, 1968, the day after Richard Nixon was elected President of the United States. (For those keeping score, I lasted twice as long as Nixon did.)

Before the Century Plaza job, I had always worked in street stores, all in choice locations with plenty of street traffic. When you work in a hotel shop, business depends on how well the hotel is doing. Ideally, if the hotel was booked at 85% capacity, we did a brisk business. The hotel has eight hundred rooms, plus a number of ballrooms, catering rooms, several up-scale restaurants and numerous shops on both the lobby and plaza levels.

Also, there are lots of high-rise buildings in Century City that provide office space to huge numbers of accountants, lawyers, doctors, stockbrokers and Indian chiefs. (Just joking about the Indian chiefs.) In addition to all that, there's the ABC Entertainment Center directly across the street from the hotel. Back then, the Entertainment Center included the Schubert Theater and twin movie theaters. Below was an underground garage for two thousand cars.

Just because there are many high-rise office buildings and an entertainment center close by doesn't mean our business was booming. We were pretty much dependent on the amount of guests staying at the hotel. You see, most of the people who worked in Century City, at the end of the day, would be eager to jump into their cars, head for home and never set foot in our store.

Fortunately, I learned the retail clothing business from experts. So it was, when I came to work at the Century Plaza, I started a customer file. For every customer I sold to, I would write his name, address, phone number, his suit size, the color suit or sport coat he purchased, his waist measurement, shirt size, shoe size—all this information on a 3x5 index card.

I would send him a "thank you" card two weeks after his purchase. In some instances, I even had his birthday indexed. Many of our customers came to Los Angeles for business and we tried to keep a close relationship with each one.

It's been said that, "When the going gets tough the tough get going." Or in my case, the tough hit the Rolodex, or my version of it. So, on quiet days when the hotel only had 50% occupancy, I would go to my customer file. I would try to figure out who would be receptive to a phone call.

Naturally, the purpose of the call was to sell something over the phone. I had the ability to look at a garment and visualize how a particular customer would look in that garment. If he was receptive, I would send the merchandise with the proper accessories, subject to his approval.

I knew in advance how the garment would fit him and assured him it would need very minor alteration. I would tell him to take it to his local tailor, send us the bill and we would reimburse him. Most of these out-of-town customers lived in cities with populations of two to three hundred thousand. The more affluent ones often belonged to a country club.

Usually, there are two leading men's clothing stores in towns of those sizes. I knew that men, like women, don't like to buy something locally and be seen at the office or club wearing the same thing as their friends. So, when I called, they knew that I had something exclusive. I would accessorize the garment with just the right shirt and tie; and, in some cases, even shoes and hosiery.

It was amazing the amount of business I was doing over the phone. We could charge merchandise to a customer's credit card or, in some cases, we had already set up charge accounts for them. I always assured them that the merchandise was sent subject to their approval.

Bob and Billy, Bob Snyder's father, had never seen anything like this before. Immodest as it sounds, I was so skillful that I very seldom had to take merchandise back. There was a gentleman in Dallas who became my best customer. I had a customer in Boise, Ann Arbor, Chicago, Revere, Massachusetts, and even as far away as San Juan, Puerto Rico.

As the manager of the store, I tried to help other salesmen do the same thing. So, that's what I did when we had the time to work our customer files. Bob Snyder showed his appreciation when I would receive my pay envelope.

Several times I received calls from customers complaining that they hadn't heard from me in six months and asked whether I had something I thought they would like, explaining that they had gotten many compliments on previous shipments. Those are the kind of complaints I loved to get. (I confess that, since I retired, I love to get compliments about my singing.)

I remember once I received a call from Barry Galloway, my Dallas customer. "Jerry," he said, "I'm invited to a Roaring Twenties party. My lady friend and I have to come dressed as they did during that era. You have all my measurements. Send me an outfit through Federal Express. And, oh yes, send a boa for my lady friend."

On my day off, I went to Hollywood and found a business that rented clothing to the movie studios. I selected just the right garment that was worn during that era and sent a boa for his girlfriend. The Hollywood store even threw in a fake revolver and a shoulder holster. I charged it to his account.

After the party, he returned the merchandise and I received a phone call thanking me. He was a huge hit at the party. I joked that maybe I ought to be a movie costume designer. He joked back, "Jerry, as your friend, definitely don't quit your day job."

CHAPTER 72

HE WALKED THE LINE, BUT IT WASN'T EASY (1978)

While this story took place in 1978, as I edit it in January, 2020, unless there's a typo on my driver's license, I just turned 98. When people ask what's the secret to longevity I often mention a few mottoes to live by, which, who knows, may account for my long life.

One is "Make the best of the cards you've been dealt." Having lived through the Great Depression, another is, "Don't feel sorry for yourself, because someone always has it worse." Fortunately, I learned early on to be happy for what I had, rather than dwell on what I didn't.

Especially to my young friends on Instagram, I tell them each day try to plan something to look forward to. Believe it or not, that's exactly how I felt about being the manager at Snyder & Son men's store in the Century Plaza Hotel. (How's that for a segue?) The truth is, I couldn't wait to open the doors each morning because I never knew what interesting and exciting people would come into our shop.

The 800-room hotel served as a lavish convention site, for, as the saying goes, doctors, lawyers, accountants and Indian chiefs. (Actually, talk about "interesting" I wish there had been an Indian chief gathering.)

This particular week was a Country Music convention. Growing up in Brooklyn in the 1930's, I knew all about the Big Band Era and Broadway musicals, but nothing about country music. I was about to learn.

As fate would have it, the first customer from the convention to enter our store was the much revered Johnny Cash, who, over his 50-year career, sold more than 90 million records. Tall, rugged and handsome, I vividly remember he was wearing a custom-tailored black silk shirt, not surprising as he was famously called "The man in black."

Apparently, Cash was in a mood to talk and I was definitely in a mood to listen. But I learned even more about him the following day from country legend Merle Haggard. (For that week at least, instead of an upscale men's store, Snyder & Son felt more like the Grand Ole Opry.)

As I would learn, Haggard was 20 when he met Cash but it wasn't exactly under ideal circumstances. It was at San Quentin Prison where Haggard was serving time for burglary.

And yet, this very first Cash prison concert, on January 1, 1958, inspired Haggard on the path to becoming a country western recording star himself. (Haggard believed that Cash identified so strongly with inmates because of his serious drug and alcohol addictions that made him feel like a prisoner.)

Later in the week June Carter-Cash, Johnny's beautiful wife, came in to buy her husband some sports shirts. I would come to find she was a five-time Grammy-winning singer, songwriter, and a member of country western royalty. (Born to Maybelle and Ezra Carter, she performed for years with her mom and sisters, Helen and Anita.)

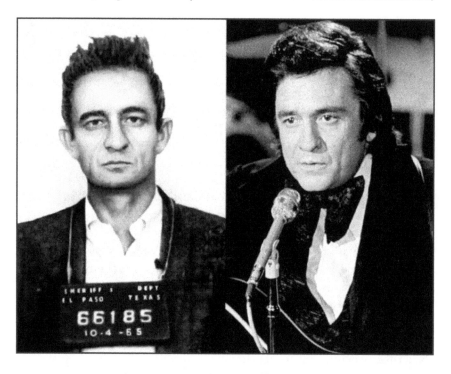

The last country star to come into our store was Sarah Ophelia Colley Cannon who performed as "Minnie Pearl." She appeared at the Grand Ole Opry from 1940 to 1991

and on the TV show Hee Haw from 1969 to 1991. Minnie's over the top, ditsy character wore a hat with the price tag still on it. But in real life, she was an elegant woman.

While I pride myself on being able to remember what famous customers bought, even decades later, all I remember was that Cash purchased two hand-painted Peter Max ties. Ironically, when the store owner, Bob Snyder, first bought the psychedelic neck wear I thought they would just gather dust, instead they sold like hotcakes. (Not sure how that expression ever got started.)

I was so impressed with Cash, years later I bought his autobiography. He was a talented and complicated man who had a big heart for the down trodden, including Native Americans. Like most country singers, Cash supported the Vietnam War, until, in 1971, he made a visit.

Cash, a patriotic veteran, and June, who would be his wife for 33 years, performed tirelessly for the troops. They also interacted with the injured and even performed in hospitals to groups as small as 10. Risking offending his politically conservative fans, Cash was so convinced our policy was wrong, he wrote a song "Singing in Vietnam Talking Blues."

Ahead of his time, another of the causes Cash embraced was prison reform, for which he testified in Congress. He even met with Richard Nixon, but was unable to persuade the president.

As with many conventions at the hotel, I met and learned from such a variety of interesting people, some of whom I'd stay in touch with for years and years. (I'm joking, but not entirely, when I wonder what it would have been like if we'd ever had that Indian Chief convention.)

CHAPTER 73

I SHOULDA BEEN A HOLLYWOOD TALENT SCOUT (1979)

While this story ends in 1979, it began in 1947. I was working at Kallen's Clothes in New York City. One of my favorite customers was a tall (6'5") exceptionally good-looking, young man, Ken Scibath, who was born in Brooklyn only 6 years after I was.

One day, as we chatted, he told me he drove a truck. Somehow that didn't compute. A good-looking guy like him, driving a truck? Not to knock truck drivers, mind you, but it seemed he could do a lot better. (And, as you might know by now, I'm not the shy type, so I told him as a compliment.)

As we chatted further, I asked if he had ever thought of becoming a model for men's clothing, or even go into acting. It never occurred to him, he said. Well, maybe I must have given him something to think about because the next time he came in, he was carrying a large leather folder. "Jerry, "I want to show you something."

He then opened the folder and, lo and behold, there was a series of professional photos of Ken modeling clothes. I was flabbergasted. He had actually taken my suggestion. He didn't quit his day job, but he explained he was modeling on a part-time basis.

The next time he paid me a visit, he told me he was doing some acting Off Broadway. Again, I was amazed and was enjoying his development almost as much as he was. Now, here is the clincher. The very next time he came into the store it was to say good-bye. What?

He explained that a talent scout from Twentieth Century Fox Studios spotted him in a show and signed him to a contract and he was leaving for Hollywood. His stage name was Ken Scott. You could have knocked me over with a feather, as the saying goes.

Exactly ten years later, I was in a movie theater and I was stunned. I actually saw Ken on the big screen! He had a major part in Stop Over Tokyo with Robert Wagner. They both played CIA agents and the locale was Japan. What a strange feeling seeing Ken up there on the screen and realizing, to a tiny degree, it was some of my doing.

Well, Ken was in many movies and television shows. I remember seeing his name several times in the Hollywood columns linking him with various starlets. He made a movie with Joanne Woodward Three Faces of Eve in 1957 in which played Joanne's second husband.

Ken was in the last ten minutes of the movie for which Joanne Woodward won an Academy Award. David Wayne played her first husband and Lee J. Cobb played the psychiatrist. After a while, however, I didn't see Ken or read about him anymore. Cut to 1979.

While working at the Century Plaza store, I happened to be looking out of the window. Watching limos and taxis pull up to the front entrance of the hotel, I noticed one of the limos was parked off on the side and a tall chauffeur was leaning against it.

Something about this fellow caught my eye. And when I took a closer look, I realized it was Ken Scott. Now mind you, I had not seen Ken in person since 1949. Over thirty years had passed. He was in his middle 50's and I had recently turned 60.

I walked up and asked him if I looked familiar. He didn't recognize me until I told him I used to sell him clothing at Kallen's Clothes. I never mentioned a word about his career because it was obvious he was no longer acting, at least full time. He looked dissipated. I hate to say it, but he had the look of someone who had an alcohol problem. We chatted briefly, and I told him to please come into the store anytime. But, sadly, he never did. In 1986, by chance, I happened to see his obituary in the L.A. Times. He passed away at 58, such a young age.

Then one day in the early 90's, I was having my car washed when I noticed a familiar-looking man waiting for his Land Rover. His car and my Lincoln were side by side. The owner of the Land Rover was none other than Robert Wagner. Again, rarely shy, I asked him if he remembered Ken Scott.

"Of course I do," he replied. "We were in a few films together and he was also in some of the Heart to Heart" episodes. I told Wagner that Ken used to drive a truck in New York City and that I was the one who put the acting bug in his head. "You're kidding?" he said in astonishment.

As we continued to chat, we both agreed that it was sad Ken was gone and his life had ended badly. But I suggested that it was a mistake to judge the full life of a person on just how it ends. I said I chose to remember Ken by what he accomplished against all odds and how many wonderful and exciting times he had working with so many talented people. Wagner seemed to like how I put it very much as we shook hands warmly and said goodbye.

Now cut to 2008 and I read in our local paper that Robert Wagner was going to be speaking at our main library discussing his recent autobiography "Pieces of My Heart." I decided to go to the event and found the commentary about his life, his work, his two marriages to Natalie Wood, her tragic death, his understandable grief and his nearly 30-year marriage to Jill St. John, all fascinating.

Afterwards I went up to him and was delighted that he remembered me and our conversation about Ken. I bought his book and had him sign it. And, now that I think of it, if he buys my book, I would be glad to sign my book for him.

CHAPTER 74

THE DAY I SOLD 1000 PAIR OF SOCKS (1980)

One of our customers at the Century Plaza Hotel shop just loved our velour socks. They came in six colors and he used to tell me he couldn't find them in any other store. Each time he would come in, he would buy a dozen pair. Back then in the 1970s, they sold for about $3.50 a pair.

Now, fast forward to November, 1980. My boss, Bob Snyder, decided to retire. At 55, he planned to attend Pepperdine University to prepare to become a psychologist. So, we had a huge retirement sale.

Shortly after the sale began, I was crossing the lobby to go to lunch at the employee cafeteria. I spotted the customer who loved the velour socks in the lobby having a cocktail. I walked over and informed him we were closing the store forever, so now would be a good time to load up on the velour socks he loved so. "Thanks for the heads up" he said. "I'll be in."

Well, he was true to his word. He came in when I got back from lunch and told me he wanted a thousand pairs of velour socks. I kept calm, as if this were an everyday occurrence. "You see," he explained, "I have four homes. My permanent residence is in Canada but I also have homes in New York City, Hawaii, and Lake Tahoe. (Not bad, huh?)

Anyway, he wanted 250 pairs of socks shipped to each address. I figured out that at $3.50 per pair, less the 20% discount from the going out of business sale, he had saved himself $700. (From my viewpoint, I just sold $2800 worth of socks!)

He gave me all four addresses and I instructed the factory to give him a variety of colors for each address and to drop ship the cartons directly to his four homes. As per our instructions, we saved him the sales tax because the socks were being shipped out of state.

I remember handing Bob Snyder the check for close to three thousand dollars explaining that I had sold a thousand pairs of socks. Bob couldn't believe it and joked, "Jerry, I think you just might have made the Guinness World Record for socks!" (Now that I think about it, it's a shame it's too late to apply to Guinness.)

As I write this, between you and me, I wonder two things: One, is that customer still alive? (Hopefully, yes.) And, two, could he have possible worn out all those socks?

CHAPTER 75

WHEN ONE DOOR CLOSES, DON'T LET IT HIT YOU IN THE BUTT (1980)

I came to work for Snyder & Sons at the Century Plaza Hotel on November 9, 1968. I worked there for twelve years. In November 1980, Bob Snyder decided to retire. He had literally grown up in the business. working in his father's store from such a young age. Now, at fifty-five, he had reached a crossroad. His lease was up for renewal and he had become very interested in studying psychology. So, we ran a retirement sale and a few months later we closed the store.

When I had come to work there in 1968, I was the sixth salesman on the floor. The hotel was only five years old and everybody wanted to stay at the Century Plaza. We had a choice location on the lobby level and, I must say, that the store itself had a certain ambiance like no store I had known. Our customers were always telling us what a pleasure it was to shop in our store. And, of course, the merchandise was top quality and upscale.

To his credit, Bob Snyder, always a "searcher" looking to evolve, enrolled in Pepperdine University and got his degree and opened an office in the interim. He divorced and met a young Mexican girl who was doing the same work. They were married and now live in Cuernevaca, Mexico where they share an office and have a young daughter. Her father owns a department store in town.

After working in the Century Plaza for twelve years, I knew all the customers and suppliers. People were telling me that I would be the right man to take over the store. I knew the business from A to Z and, thank my lucky stars, I had sufficient capital.

Instead of six salesmen, we were down to three and I could see where the men's clothing business was headed, downhill. I also reasoned that Bob Snyder was no dummy.

As fate would have it, about that time I received a call from Dick Caruso, who was managing his father's store in Santa Monica. He offered me a job and, knowing I lived in Santa Monica, he reminded me that not only would he pay well, I could walk home for lunch. It was an offer I couldn't refuse. And, as I look back, I'm so glad I took it. I really do believe as one door closes another door opens. You just have to look for it.

CHAPTER 76

MY MOBSTER CUSTOMER GOT WHACKED (1983)

While the "customer" in my title met his untimely demise (or "timely" depending on your point of view) in 1983, the beginning of the story goes back to when I worked at Snyder and Son men's store in the Century Plaza Hotel. It was there I came in contact with all kinds of people, some famous, some infamous. This story is about the latter.

One afternoon, a group of four Teamster Union officials came into the store. The group included William Presser, who I later discovered, was in charge of the union pension fund. Jimmy Hoffa had designated Presser to be in charge of the fund while he, Hoffa, was in prison.

Another in the group was Alan Dorfman. (Whose character is featured in the movie "The Irishman") Apparently, he was go-between with the Mafia Dons and whoever was in charge of the pension. The pension fund consisted of hundreds of millions of dollars. So, you can be sure Hoffa, Presser, Dorfman, and the lawyer for the Teamsters, Alvin Barron, were all dipping their mitts in that huge pot of gold. (What could go wrong there?)

Some of the hotels in Las Vegas were built with Teamster pension money. That included the La Costa Hotel and Country Club in Carlsbad near San Diego. La Costa was a spa where the guys who were "connected" would go to relax.

William Presser was a rather large man. Actually "rather large" doesn't quite cover it. (Pun intended.) You see he needed double extra large in shirts to "cover it," meaning his huge belly. We couldn't sell him a suit or sports coat because he needed size 54 and we only stocked up to size 48. I did manage to sell him shoes, hosiery and shirts.

Before he went to prison, Hoffa had put an Irishman, Frank Fitzsimmons, in power to take his place with the understanding that when Jimmy was released he would get his job back. Once I realized who these people were, I went to our local library to read up on the Teamsters. It made for some fascinating, albeit disturbing reading.

Nixon was President and, through intermediaries, Hoffa told him that if he would agree to commute Hoffa's sentence, Hoffa would arrange for a hefty campaign contribution toward Nixon's reelection. (With what we know of Nixon, he seemed particularly interested in campaign contributions, even more than the average politician and that's saying something.)

Eventually, Nixon agreed to pardon Hoffa under one condition. He told Hoffa that if he was released from prison he must never try to get his old job back as Teamster's Union president.

Curiously, the mob was getting more money out of the Teamster's pension fund than when Hoffa was top dog. The mob was doing great with Fitzsimmons and they wanted to keep it that way. So, you know the rest.

A day later, Dorfman bought the farm.

In 1975, they killed Hoffa shortly after he was released and the mystery is that no one knows how they disposed of his body as he was never found. Jack Nicholson starred as Hoffa in the movie of the same name and he was brilliant, as was the movie, in my humble opinion.

So there I was chatting with all these underworld characters. One day Presser came into the store with his son Jerry who was even larger in girth than his father.

Jerry eventually became Teamster president after they got Fitzsimmons out. And from newspaper reports, after Jerry Presser died it was reported he was acting as an informant for the FBI.

The truth is, they were all a bunch of thugs. Even Alvin Barron, the Teamster's lawyer, went to prison for a couple of years. As for Alan Dorfman, on January 20, 1983, he was found in an alley in Chicago with a bullet in the back of his head. Apparently, he had gotten himself in trouble with someone high up in the Mafia. It's no secret those guys play rough.

Meanwhile, I remember William Presser telling me that I should call him if any sport shirts came into the store in double extra large. Well, it happened we received a shipment from one of our suppliers and, after looking them over carefully, I realized that he would like three or four of the shirts. I called the number he gave me but apparently it was his office phone, answered by one of his assistants.

When I told him why I was calling, she said, "He's in Florida. I'll give you a number where he can be reached." I dialed that number and Presser answered and was irate. "How did you get this number?" he demanded. I told him, "Someone in your office gave it to me." But he continued to be furious.

I later reasoned that he probably had a condo down there bought with Teamster pension money and wanted to keep a very low profile. The fact is, the FBI was starting to close in on all the corruption that was going on.

In the clothing business for 50 years, I always wanted to make a sale. But I definitely didn't want to get my head blown off in the process. After that rather menacing call, he never asked and I certainly never sent him any more shirts.

CHAPTER 77

THE MILLION DOLLAR MERMAID (1984)

I've included this story at the insistence of my editor who feels it's essential for two reasons. One, it's about my remarkable friendship with Esther Williams, a world class competitive swimmer who would have surely won a Gold Medal at the 1940 London Olympics but for the outbreak of WWII which canceled the games and her dreams of Olympic Gold were shattered.

Bravely picking up the pieces, Esther turned her beauty and talent into becoming a major movie star in the 1940's and 1950's. Via her many successful films, she swam into the hearts of Americans everywhere.

Reason #two from my editor: he feels how I inadvertently happened to cross paths with Esther which built into a genuine friendship, epitomizes my "easy to get along with" personality. (The point is, if, after reading it, you don't care for this chapter, feel free to blame it on my editor.

Now, finally, for those too young to know about Esther Williams, her rise to movie stardom is a Hollywood legend. Esther was born in Inglewood, a suburb of Los Angeles, in 1921, the youngest of 5 children of Louis and Bula Williams. Louis was s sign painter, Bula was a psychologist.

At 5'8", Esther was not only uncommonly and naturally beautiful, she was a remarkably gifted swimmer. She set multiple national and regional records and won 3 U.S. National Championships while still in her teens. In 1940, when the games were cancelled Esther joined Billy Rose's Aquacade, glamorous swimming musicals which featured elaborate performances with synchronized swimming and diving.

Esther swam alongside Olympic Gold medal winner and Tarzan movie star, Johnny Weissmuller. (Another name I fear young people won't recognize.) Suffice it to say, Esther was spotted by MGM and the rest was movie history.

From 1945 to 1949, Williams had at least one film among the 20 highest-grossing movies of the year. In 1952, she appeared in her only bio pic as Australian swimming star Annette Kellerman in Million Dollar Mermaid. This became Esther's nickname at MGM, and also the title of her best-selling autobiography in 2000.

Right about now you're probably wondering how did I befriend Esther Williams in the first place. The year was 1985. I was a salesman at Mike Caruso's men's shop in Santa Monica. I had just made a rather large sale and was helping the customer carry his bags and boxes to his car.

We loaded everything into his trunk and. as he drove off, a well-dressed elderly woman I assumed was in her 70's (she was 83) approached me. "I know you, from somewhere" she said authoritatively, even though she couldn't remember from where. Trying to be polite, I answered her questions as she tried to place me. Actually, I was kind of curious myself.

As nice as she was beautiful.

"I've got it!" she blurted out. "You grew up in Brighton Beach, right?" "Why yes," I responded. She continued, "I saw you win a handball tournament at the beach club." I had to laugh because, amazingly, she was right and I was 18 when I won that tournament. Here I thought I had a good memory, but hers put mine to shame.

The woman, Ruth Bell, was pretty damn sharp. In any event, we had a fun few minutes catching up and agreed to have lunch to continue and picked a date to do it.

Days later, at lunch we chatted away until she came up with an idea. It seems her son was married to Esther Williams who was planning a big Memorial Day party at her Beverly Hills house. Ruth was invited and since we both lived in Santa Monica, she suggested I come and drive her. And she also extended the invitation to my mother. I was a big fan of Williams as was mom, so I eagerly agreed.

Williams' 3-story house in Beverly Hills had a breathtaking city view. And the party was fantastic. Esther met my mother, who was 98 and took an instant liking to her outgoing personality.

At one point, Esther took me into her den to show me various photos from her movie career, including one of her and Clark Gable. She was very proud that, in her first screen test, it had been Gable, already a big star, who the studio had read lines with her. You couldn't help but be smitten with Williams who was a wonderful combination of being down to earth and yet had such elegance.

Over the years I was invited to Esther's house numerous times. Once she gave me a copy of her autobiography "The Million Dollar Mermaid," and also a few video cassettes of her most famous movies. I still have them to this day.

Despite all her success, Williams had more than her share of trauma. She broke her neck filming a 115 ft dive off a tower during a climactic musical number for the film Million Dollar Mermaid and was in a body cast for seven months. She subsequently recovered, although she continued to suffer headaches as a result of the accident.

Also, Williams' many hours submerged in a studio tank resulted in ruptured eardrums numerous times. She also nearly drowned after not being able to find the trap door in the ceiling of a tank. The walls and ceiling were painted black and the trap door blended in. Williams was pulled out only because a member of the crew realized the door was not opening.

And Williams' marital life was star-crossed, to say the least. She was married 4 times and her various husbands' track records were checkered, to put it kindly. Without mentioning names, one husband stole $10 million from her. Another, was so possessive he insisted she quit making movies as he basically wanted to "own" her. He collected every photo of her with her leading men and burned them. "Those are my memories!" she shouted. He responded, "I can't stand thinking of other men having touched you."

Meanwhile, I was privileged and honored to be invited to Esther's 80th birthday party. Esther was confined to a wheelchair and yet she was still radiant as always. I loved being at the party. There I was Jerry from working class Brighton Beach, hob-nobbing with all these glamorous people I've seen on the big screen my whole life. With all the celebrities and all in such a festive mood chatting away, I was like a kid in a candy shop. (Except for the small detail I hadn't been a kid for 60 years or more.)

I immensely enjoyed my friendship with Esther who confided in me so often I was always flattered and always remained a true friend. It was truly an honor for me. And to think, it might not have ever happened if I hadn't won a handball tournament when I was 18. Go figure.

CHAPTER 78

DENNIS WAS ENGAGED TO LIZ FOR...
1 MINUTE! (1985)

In Brooklyn seven decades ago there was a very popular cafeteria on King Highway at the corner of East 16th Street called Dubrow's. The food was tasty and reasonably priced. After a Saturday night on the town, we would all stop at Dubrow's for a midnight snack and talk about anything and everything.

One of the younger fellows in the group was Dennis Stein, whom we used to call "Dennis the Menace." An unusually handsome kid, his father owned Stein's, a men's clothing store at the Sheepshead Bay Station of the BMT Line. I was several years older than he was and also in the men's clothing business. I worked on 7th Avenue in the heart of the Garment District.

As the years passed, I became manager and Dennis was now buying clothes for his father's store. Occasionally, he would stop in our store for ideas as to what was "hot" in the market place. You see, we were located a great distance away from Stein's, so we really didn't compete with each other.

Dennis's idol was Frank Sinatra and he was determined that some day, somehow, he would befriend Frank. Dennis found out where Sinatra liked to drink with his buddies, a darkly-lit bar called Jilly's in Manhattan's theater district and he started going there.

Reportedly, once Dennis picked up a big bar tab that Sinatra had run up and gradually ingratiated himself with Frank and his cronies. Through this connection, I suppose, he was invited to parties where he would come in contact with some of the biggest names in Hollywood.

There was no name bigger than Elizabeth Taylor. She was in between husbands. (Having been married 8 times, I suppose she was often "in between husbands.") In any event, apparently Dennis and Elizabeth became an item for the gossip columnists. I read that before he met Elizabeth Taylor he had been going out with Joan Collins.

When I moved to Los Angeles in 1963, I lost contact with the guys in Brooklyn. So, you can imagine my surprise when one day, standing at the checkout counter of Von's Supermarket, I saw a photo of Dennis and Elizabeth Taylor on the front page of the National Inquirer in December, 1984.

Naturally, I bought the paper and read that Dennis and Elizabeth were engaged to be married. On one of the inside pages was a picture of Dennis and Liz sitting at a table in Chasen's Restaurant with Gregory Peck and his wife. Imagine! "Dennis the Menace" about to marry one of the most famous actresses in the world, true Hollywood royalty, Elizabeth Taylor.

I read that Elizabeth had Dennis as her guest at her villa in Gatschat, Switzerland, and that's where he popped the question. The story continued on about how Dennis was divorced from his first wife and was manufacturing jeans in South Korea.

Liz gave back the ring but kept the stone.

Well, surprise, surprise, the marriage never took place. In February 1985, I saw another National Enquirer that revealed the two had "an amicable break-up." The article went on to say, "Taylor, 52, no longer wears the sapphire and diamond engagement ring Stein gave her when she accepted his marriage proposal in mid-December after a whirlwind two-month courtship."

The article didn't say if Elizabeth kept the engagement ring. I was reminded of what Zsa Zsa Gabor said about one of her many engagements that fell through, when she was asked if she gave the ring back. "I always give the ring back, but I also always keep the stone."

The next thing I read was that Elizabeth had married truck driver Larry Fortensky at, of all places, Michael Jackson's Neverland Ranch. This last thing I heard about Dennis was that he had some kind of executive job with Revlon.

Too bad Liz didn't marry Dennis because she could have had free makeup for the rest of her life. Of course given, she had an estimated net worth of $600 million, free makeup might not have been such an irresistible perk.

CHAPTER 79

MY NEIGHBOR, THE KID TV STAR (1987)

Mom and I shared a twelfth floor ocean view apartment on Ocean Avenue in Santa Monica, the Pacific Plaza Apartments. New tenants, newlyweds named the Tarsitanos, moved into an apartment on the same floor, only three doors away. Ralph was a professional singer, having entertained in nightclubs and cruise ships and Tammy was an aspiring actress.

About two years later, Tammy gave birth to Luke. He was an adorable little boy whom you couldn't help but love. When he was barely three, Tammy found an agency that specialized in placing children in TV commercials. And, soon Luke was appearing in numerous commercials.

When Luke turned four, Steven Spielberg, the Hollywood movie director (as opposed to Steven Spielberg who works at the post office?) was looking for a little boy to play the lead part in a TV series called Fudge. Luke was one of the first to be auditioned but Spielberg would go on to audition hundreds of other 4-year-olds. And then, fortuitously for the Tarsitano family, he then chose Luke, his original favorite, to star in the series.

It seems Spielberg, who was nearly a billionaire at the time, owned a production company. This TV series was sold to ABC and Luke, at age four, was suddenly starring in a television series! Luke even was a guest on the Jay Leno Show, only that didn't go so swimmingly.

Luke was his usual, precocious self when Jay asked him what he wanted to be when he grew up. "A paleontologist!" he blurted out and the audience was hysterical. Under the heading "kids say the darnedest things," a slight problem occurred, however, when Luke observed that Jay had "an awfully big chin." Fellow guest, Jon Stewart, grabbed his forehead as if to say, "Uh oh." Jay pretended to be offended causing more laughs, so no harm was done.

Luke ages 5 & 21, me old & older lol.

Meanwhile, the series aired on ABC Channel 7 every Saturday morning. Mom and I never failed to watch. A natural-born actor, Luke was sensational in the part. The program ran for two successful seasons and could have continued if not for what happened. You see Walt Disney, Inc. bought ABC.

Apparently, someone high up in the Disney organization decided that, now that they owned a major TV station, they would show some of the shows they had developed for TV and Fudge was canceled. Not that Disney ever asked my opinion, but that always seemed to be a major blunder. Believe me, the replacement was nothing, and a great show was knocked off the air.

After that, Luke auditioned many times, but after what happened, he understandably developed a distaste for show business. He did get parts in a few shows but it was never the same. Meanwhile, his dad wasn't in the best of health, so money became a bigger issue.

Fudge, the TV series, was still being shown in many countries around the world and royalty checks were coming in, so that helped. Had the show been able to run a full five years, it could have gone into syndication and that would have been a boon for the Tarsitanos.

During those two years, Luke made return appearances on the Jay Leno Show. It was such fun the neighbors to see a stretch limousine drive up to the entrance of our apartment building. The chauffeur would hold the door open for Luke and he would climb in with his parents, bound for the NBC Studios.

Jay Leno always presented Luke with a gift of some kind and, of course, the money came in handy. But in the end, a golden opportunity had been dashed by some TV executive who, in my humble opinion, didn't know what the hell he was doing. Unfortunately, Luke never got another break. But maybe it was for the best.

Sadly, his dad passed away in 2007. He had been a very devoted father and Tammy and Luke miss him very much to this day. But, as I update this story in 2019, there is terrific news. Luke graduated from Loyola Marymount University, having majored in political science. And today he's an up and coming music producer and has already experienced considerable success.

Tammy just finished a children's book that's currently at the publishers in the process of being edited. So all's well that ends well.

CHAPTER 80

RUMORS TO THE CONTRARY, OLD AGE CAN BE FUN (1991-2019)

To help support my mother and younger brother, from age 12, I was a "serious" kid who always had at least one job and as many as three at any time. My young friends would make good natured fun and call me a "super hero." The truth was I was proud to help my family and took pride in it, but, in many ways, I clearly did not have a typical childhood. Starting at age 70, I've been having, what I suppose you could call, a second childhood.

Obviously, with old age, there are many challenges, including health. Frankly, I've had more than my share of health issues including: quadruple heart bypass, two hip replacements, two carpal tunnel, double hernia and prostate surgery. (Though not all in the same week.)

When I turned the big 70, however, I retired after fifty-eight years of work, being unemployed for a total of two weeks in all that time! But from 70 on, I did what I wanted and when I wanted. Or, as I joked, I became a "septuagenarian teenager." (I have an uneasy feeling that line may be funnier in person.)

At the top of the list of my newly-found interests was world travel as I went on six different luxury cruises. Next was going to the movies, the theater and lectures; taking classes at the Emeritus College and, in general, making sure every day I had something fun planned. Curiously, this big change all began with the first time I sang in public.

One of the reasons we lived in the apartment on Ocean Avenue in Santa Monica was because of the Senior Center across the street so Mom could socialize with people her age. Also, she loved to sing and they had a sing-a-long every Tuesday morning. I would bring Mom to the class and they would hand out song sheets that contained songs from the 20's on up to the 70's. That would last half an hour and then those who wanted to would sing a solo accompanied by a piano.

Mom and I would sing along with the others and found it to be very enjoyable. Mom always had a good voice and a fine ear for music. I clearly must have inherited her love of music. I always would sing while in the shower. As everyone knows, acoustics are great in the shower where it sounded like I had a decent voice.

The only problem is, if I wanted someone's opinion of my singing ability, I could hardly ask them to jump in the shower with me. An additional problem was I had a very limited repertoire. By heart, I only knew "God Bless America," "The Star Spangled Banner" and "Chattanooga Choo-Choo."

At the senior center one day, the mistress of ceremonies asked if there was someone in the audience who would like to do a solo because one of our regular soloists didn't show up. At age 70 I was the "kid" in the group so she more picked me than I volunteered. Either way, I went up front.

When asked what I'd like to sing, I didn't have much choice. I couldn't very well perform the "Star Spangled Banner," or "God Bless America," so "Chattanooga Choo-Choo" was it.

For those not familiar (probably everybody under 70) "Chattanooga Choo Choo" is a 1941 song originally recorded as a big band/swing tune by Glenn Miller. For trivia buffs, in 1942 it was the first song to receive a gold record for its sales of 1.2 million copies!

While I had never sang in public before and was quite nervous, believe it or not, after I finished, I got a very enthusiastic round of applause. (And may have liberated me from only singing in the shower!) The mistress of ceremonies said, "From now on you're going to sing every Tuesday."

Common sense dictated I couldn't sing "Chattanooga Choo Choo" every week or somebody would literally put me on the Chattanooga Choo Choo. So I was forced to learn new songs. Like Mom, I was blessed with a good memory, so every week I'd memorize and sing a different song.

In two years I had developed a respectable repertoire. Also, the nervousness that first time was long gone. In fact, I developed a little ham in me. (Okay, maybe more than a little.) I had enough confidence, that, when I discovered each year the senior club put on a talent show, I decided to enter.

The shows were held at the library auditorium. The theater had 225 seats and every seat was occupied. I remember seeing people lining up along the walls. I still have videos of all the shows I participated in. Immodest as it sounds, I was one of the best singers five years in a row. The reality, of course, this was just a local contest. I wanted to see how I would fare in a bigger setting.

So it was, that when it was announced there was going to be city-wide auditions to see who was the best male and female "senior singer" in all of Los Angeles, I didn't hesitate. I entered auditions in Santa Monica, Hollywood and the Fairfax District and kept moving up the ladder.

Finally, on the day of the final concert I sang "If I Were A Rich Man" from Fiddler on The Roof. I won first prize as the best male senior singer in Los Angeles. I was given a certificate and an envelope that contained a blue ribbon that said "1st Prize", and also a twenty dollar bill. I joked to friends, "Now I really am a rich man."

I soon found myself singing in public whenever there were contests. I didn't care that much if I won, it was just so much fun, it became a passion. It also opened other doors for me.

The "success" I had with singing emboldened me to try other things, among them traveling. I started with a cruise to Turkey and Greece and wound up taking five others, including to Tahiti, Australia and South America.

On the cruise ships almost always they had amateur talent contests that I almost always entered and rather fearlessly, if I do say so. It was like, "I'm old, what difference does it make how well I do?" Musically, I was living like the Nike logo, "Just do it."

Again, I guess because of my age, I've been written about in newspapers numerous times; I've auditioned for and appeared in theatrical productions; I've been interviewed on two podcasts and I take 3 classes at Emeritus College, all in subjects I love: "Current Events," "Film Studies" and "Singing Instruction."

Yes, even at 98, I'd say that I haven't had this much fun since I was a teenager, except that I'm actually having more fun now. Go figure. (And you could say I owe it all to "Chattanooga Choo Choo.")

CHAPTER 81

STREISAND, GOULD, ELVIS AND MOM
(1994)

Having been a music lover since I was a child (a mere 90 years ago), and since I have a passion for singing, it should be no surprise that I have some favorite singers. At the top has to be Barbra Streisand whose music I've listened to so much I feel like I know her personally. Under "Kevin Bacon Six Degrees of Separation" rules, I'm only 1 degree away from Barbra and I'll explain why.

As I mentioned earlier, in 2007, I took a 26-day vacation cruise on the Queen Mary. The ship left from Port Everglades in Fort Lauderdale and went all the way to South America. It passed through the Panama Canal, which was quite an exciting adventure for me.

The Queen Mary was 918 feet long and I had great fun exploring every foot. One of the featured entertainers on the cruise was Roslyn Kind, Barbra Streisand's half sister. I often watched her perform and she was consistently terrific. She's also an actress, a songwriter and has performed on Broadway and other venues going back to her teenage days. (If only that family had some talent!)

No matter how large a cruise ship is, it tends to be intimate in the sense everyone is stuck on board. As a result you tend to see folks over and over throughout the day. I was lucky enough to befriend Roslyn and she was kind enough to talk about herself and Barbra and a variety of other subjects. We hit if off instantly because she's far from shy, and so am I. (Though I admit I had to control myself to not ask too many questions.)

As everyone knows, Barbra is married to actor James Brolin and they celebrated their twenty-first anniversary in 2019. But Barbra's first husband was famed actor Elliott Gould as the two were married from 1963 to 1971. They had one child, Jason Gould, who, believe it or not, will be 53 in December. Jason's a talented actor, writer, producer and singer, which should be no surprise given his parents.

As it happens, Elliott Gould was born in Brooklyn and so was I. He's one of my favorite actors going back to "M.A.S.H," for which he was nominated for a Golden Globe. He also was an Oscar-Nominee for "Bob & Carol, Ted & Alice."

More recently Elliott's been in the fantastically successful "Ocean's 11" trilogy, for which he got rave reviews for his inventive characterization of Reuben Tishkoff, a flamboyant business kingpin. In 2018, Gould was featured in "Ocean's 8," starring Sandra Bullock. Here's something many movie buffs might not know. In 1971, was reportedly cast over Paul Newman and Robert Redford, Gould was hired by famed Swedish director, Ingmar Bergman, in "The Touch," and considers it among the greatest honors of his career.

But there were plenty of other movies of Gould's I loved, including: "California Split," "The Long Goodbye," "A Bridge Too Far," "The Silent Partner," "American History X," "Nashville," and "Little Murders," which he also produced. Staggering as it sounds, to date Elliott has been in 186 movies. If you're keeping count, that's a helluva lot!

Elliott & Mom solving world problems.

My mother was an even bigger fan of Gould's. So it was one afternoon when she and I were in the 3rd Street Promenade (Mom was an avid people watcher and that was her favorite spot) she spotted Elliott enter Johnny Rocket's restaurant.

"Was that Elliott Gould?" my mother, 97 and in a wheelchair, asked excitedly. I hesitated to answer because I had a funny feeling she was going to ask me to ask Elliott if she could meet him. My funny feeling was, of course, correct.

I went into Johnny Rocket's and approached Elliott who, luckily, hadn't ordered yet. In fact, he hadn't even sat down. I say "luckily" because I wouldn't have disturbed him if he was already eating. The truth is, he couldn't have been nicer.

Somewhat reluctantly, I explained that my mother was a huge fan and asked if maybe he would say hello. We would have waited until after he was done eating, that's how much Mom wanted to talk to him. But he insisted on meeting her right away.

And the two hit if off instantly as I stayed in the background. (I almost never took a camera with me but that day I had put it in Mom's bag.) In fact, I didn't actually hear what they were saying because I wanted to take a photo. I also didn't want to cut into their time, but I could tell Mom was thrilled and Elliott seemed to be enjoying the interaction.

After about fifteen minutes, Elliott said goodbye to Mom who was on cloud 9. He headed toward the entrance of Johnny Rocket's when I thanked him for his kindness to my mother. "No, thank you," he said graciously, "your mother is a delight."

Curious as I could be, I sat down next to Mom. "What did you ask him?" I inquired. "Well, the first thing I said was 'Is there any chance you and Barbra will get back together?'" (This was long before she married Brolin.)

"Mom, you didn't really ask that, did you?" "I certainly did," she said proudly. "And he answered that they would always be family because they had a child together."

But, as with many of these chapters, there's more to the story. A good friend of mine, a Santa Monica writer, happens to be friends with Elliott. For purpose of this book, I asked if he would ask Elliott if, by any chance, he remembers that encounter with my mother. And, amazingly enough, he did. Kind of.

What Elliott said was the only other person who ever asked so boldly if he and Barbra would get back together was...ready for this? Elvis Presley!

Upon meeting Gould for the first time, Presley had said, "You and Barbra are two of my favorite people. So why don't you guys get back together?" Gould said Presley went on and on (which hopefully Mom didn't do) until Gould finally joked, "Elvis, shuddup already."

In fact Gould said to my friend, "That should be the title of my memoir, if I ever write one." (He absolutely should. he's had such an interesting life and career.)

So call it "a small world" or maybe even "beshert," Yiddish for "meant to happen." So, as it turns out of all the people in the world, Mom had something in common with Elvis. She would have just loved that.

CHAPTER 82

ALI, HE WAS THE GREATEST
(1974 & 1997)

A great many prominent people came into the store at the Century Plaza Hotel during the twelve years I worked there. I still remember my first day on the job my boss, Billy Snyder, telling me that I must never ask any of celebrities for an autograph. I understood completely, however, and call me wacky, at home and after work, I did keep a list of these famous people, which I have to this day.

We kept our store open seven days a week. On Sunday, the hours were from 11 A.M. until 4 P.M. Our regular cashier was off on Sundays, so we had another cashier on that day named Grace. She was about 5'10" very good looking and athletic. I remember telling her when I hired her, "One of the exciting aspects of the job is that we never know who might walk into the store."

As it happened, on her very first Sunday, Muhammad Ali, who many pundits believe was the greatest heavyweight boxer of all time, entered the store. This was early in 1971. Ali was not in a good mood and I attributed that to his "legal" struggles.

For those too young to remember on April 29, 1967, Ali, at the peak of his physical prowess, was stripped of his heavyweight crown because he refused to serve in the Armed Forces. At the time we were at war with North Vietnam and Ali, a Muslim, declared that he was a conscientious objector. But, on June 20, 1967, Ali was convicted of draft evasion, sentenced to five years in prison, fined $10,000 and banned from boxing for three years.

Ali stayed out of prison as his case was appealed. Then, on June 28, 1971, the U.S. Supreme Court, ruled unanimously, overturning the lower court decision.

When Ali came into our store he was 31 and still very good looking, so much so I thought our cashier was going to faint. He didn't buy much that day but it was a thrill to see him up close like that. Good mood or not, Ali was remarkably charismatic.

Now, fast forward to 1997, twenty-three years later. Mom and I lived at the Pacific Plaza Apartments building. Mom was nearing her one hundredth birthday. We were leaving the building on this particular morning and, I saw a black man walk past the entrance and continue up Ocean Avenue. I recognized him immediately. It was Ali!

When I told Mom who he was, she yelled, "Muhammad Ali!" He stopped walking and turned toward us. I said, "Muhammad, this is the second time I've been this close to you." "When was the first time?" he asked. I told him that I had waited on him at the Century Plaza Hotel's menswear shop.

He was very gracious and friendly. I shook hands with him and he bent over and kissed Mom on the cheek. He took out some literature from inside his jacket pocket that had to do with the Muslim religion. He then autographed it for us. We continued walking toward the corner of Ocean Avenue and Broadway.

I could see by the way he walked that he wasn't well. He spoke slowly, too. I remembered reading an article about him in the newspaper in which they said his health had deteriorated because of all the blows he took to his head in the ring, especially in the later stages of his career when he should have retired.

On the corner of Broadway and Ocean Avenue there was a bar. Standing outside was an African-American man and when he saw Ali, he yelled into the bar, "Hey, Muhammad Ali is out here!" The bar emptied out immediately and there must have been a dozen men surrounding the ex-champ. Mike Tyson was now the heavyweight champ and Muhammad was asked when he was going to take on Tyson.

"When I get rid of this," he said, and pointed to his belly. Then one of the black guys started to spar with him. It was sad to see the former champion all those years later in the shape he was and yet, he was still playful.

On June 3, 2016, at the age of 74, Ali passed away and it seemed like the whole country mourned. Actually, much of the whole world mourned. Deservedly so. Go to YouTube and type "Billy Crystal's Eulogy for Ali." It's funny, moving and just so human. (Hey, if I find it on YouTube at 98, you can do it!)

CHAPTER 83

MOM TURNS 100! (1997)

For Mom's 100th birthday I threw a grand party befitting the auspicious occasion. It was held at the Double Tree Hotel, in Santa Monica, and I invited 60 of Mom's closest relatives and friends. I also invited Esther Williams who declined but with such grace, "Jerry this is about your Mom and I don't want to be any kind of distraction."

I hired a professional singer named Arlene Simone. (She had married Neil Simon's brother, Danny, but when they divorced she took the last name "Simone.") Having brought her own pianist for accompaniment, Arlene sang many of Mom's favorite tunes.

I also hired a photographer who, in addition to taking photos, went from table to table with a microphone asking the guests for the wonderful memories they had of Mom. It was truly touching. All in all, the food was delicious, the gifts were thoughtful and there so much love in the air that Mom had the terrific time she so richly deserved.

This probably sounds like the start of a joke, but a funny thing did happen at the party. My niece Heidi took out a photo someone had taken of her on a cruise ship standing next to news commentator and TV host, George Stephanopolous. (His last name could be used in a spelling bee.) As she passed the photo around everyone recognized him but couldn't remember his name. That is, until the photo arrived in Mom's hand.

"Oh, that's George Stephanopolous" Mom said casually. This on the occasion of her 100th birthday! (Talk about a sharp mind) Well, everyone broke up laughing.

A couple of weeks after the big party, something unusual happened in relation to Mom's 100th birthday. Rosalie, the director of the Israel Levin Senior Center we belonged to, called Mom and me into her office. She explained that she had received a phone call from a film production company, which was making a documentary on aging, especially seniors who were 100+ and still of sound mind.

Mom definitely fit both categories. She was still so mentally sharp that, among other feats, she was able to sing a great many songs and recite poems strictly from memory.

"Nettie," Rosalie said, "when you go home you're going to receive a call from a woman who will interview you over the phone." Hours later back at our apartment, sure enough, the phone rang. Mom answered it and the woman on the other end began interviewing her. I listened in on the bedroom phone.

After fifteen minutes, the woman said, "I think you would be a great subject for our documentary. I promise that we will be in touch in about three weeks."

A month went by and no call. I told Mom to forget all about it if they hadn't called by then. Then a week later, the phone rang and it was Emory Horvath, the producer of the documentary. With Mom's blessing, he conducted an interview and I again listened in on the other phone. After twenty minutes, he told Mom that he definitely wanted her to be in his documentary.

Never shy, Mom spoke up, "How much do you pay?" There was a long pause before Horvath responded, "Mrs. Rosenblum, we don't pay people to appear in documentaries." "And why not?" Mom responded, to which he replied, Does Jacques Cousteau pay the fish?"

"I don't know about fish," Mom said. "but I want to get paid. I've been in other documentaries and I always got paid." (Mom could be a tough negotiator.) "Hold the wire," Horvath said. And a minute later he was back. "We found fifty dollars for you," he said hopefully.

At this point, I finally intervened. I explained that we were flattered that he would consider Mom for his documentary, knowing he had called people all over the United States. That said, we would have to beg off.

I told him Mom was not in the best of health and having a film crew in our small apartment, moving furniture around and Mom being under hot lights wouldn't be good for her. I said, "Mr. Horvath, if her doctor was here I'm sure he would advise her not to go through with this project. " Mr. Horvath was disappointed but he understood completely. The less stress for Mom, the better. I felt it was my responsibility to look out for her welfare.

As for the documentary, the irony is Mom would have killed to be in it, though it might have been the cause of her demise. (Ah, the lure of show business.)

CHAPTER 84

IN LOS ANGELES A PARKING SPOT IS TO DIE FOR... ALMOST! (1998)

Among Mom's favorite food was the stuffed cabbage at Cantor's Restaurant on Fairfax, so one Saturday I drove her there. At that time, she was confined to a wheelchair. In front of the restaurant, they had a "load" and "unload" zone for three-minute parking. I parked and set up her wheelchair and wheeled her into the restaurant. I was helped to a table by the maître d' and set Mom up comfortably with the understanding that we'd order when I returned from parking the car.

Just as I was getting into my car, the car behind me was starting to pull out. I very quickly turned on the ignition and, as soon as the spot became vacant, I started to back in. Just then, as I checked the rear view mirror, I saw a Volkswagen racing down the street trying to claim the same spot.

Almost simultaneously, as I pulled into the spot first, his front bumper touched my rear bumper, though there was no damage. I got out of my car and he got out of his. He was easily thirty years younger and 30 pounds heavier than I was. "That was my spot!" he yelled as his eyes bulged out.

When he said, "You already had a spot!" I explained the spot I left was for loading and unloading only. But in L.A. logically "explaining" when it comes to a parking spot is apparently only effective if you're also packing a gun.

By this time, a crowd of people had gathered expecting a fight to break out. I thought to myself, "Do I want to tangle with this nut-cake?" Just then, he pushed me, a 76-year-old man. Thankfully, I remained calm, "Mister, I came to Cantor's to have lunch with my 100-year-old mother. I'm going into the restaurant to have a good meal and you can do whatever you want." To my surprise, the crowd applauded and shamed him. (Good for them!)

I then left him standing there, more frustrated than ever and even embarrassed for being such an obnoxious bully. I joined Mom and never told her what had just happened. After the meal, I drove home and forgot all about the incident. By the way, as always, the stuffed cabbage was delicious!

P.S. Sadly Mom passed away in November, 1999 but she had a long and wonderful life full of love. Having been born in 1897, if she had lived six more weeks, she'd have lived in three different centuries. I miss her to this day.

CHAPTER 85

CUT TO THE CHASE! (2001)

After I fully recuperated from a hip replacement on my right side, I moved from the retirement home where I was living and into a garden apartment in Brentwood. Up to that point, I had been driving a Lincoln Continental Mark IV that had belonged to Mike Caruso, my former boss at Caruso's men's store in Santa Monica. He purchased it brand new in 1982 and I bought it from his widow in 1987, as she, borrowing from The Godfather, "made me an offer, I couldn't refuse."

The Lincoln was in mint condition with only 17.000 miles and I confess it was fun to drive around in a luxury car, especially with Mom, like we were rich folk. (Mom actually saw her first car in 1907 in Minsk, Russia and came running home to excitedly tell her mother, in Yiddish, she saw a wagon going down the street "un a faird," meaning "without a horse pulling it!)

Finally, in 2001, I decided to donate the car to the Salvation Army and replaced it with a leased Mercury Marquis. It was beautiful, much smaller and handled like a dream. I lived one year in Brentwood and then was notified that an apartment in Santa Monica I had applied for two years earlier was ready for occupancy. Things were looking up!

The only drawback was that I would have to wait about another two years before I would be eligible for a parking spot in the building. I moved with the understanding that I would have to find parking on the street.

As it happens, I'm a very careful driver and, in 74 years of driving, knock wood, have had only one accident. (It wasn't my fault and was only a minor fender bender.) So, this particular Thursday, about noon, I was going to my car to drive to my

Emeritus College singing class. The car was parked at the curb just twenty feet away from the entrance to my building.

As I was crossing the threshold of the entrance, I looked to my left and saw a big furniture moving truck barreling down the street. Moments later, to my horror, it side-swiped my car and continued down the street as if nothing had happened.

Another truck was parked in the middle of the street as the driver was making a delivery to our building. He told me to call the police but I asked him if he would for me because "I'm going after the S.O.B." (In retrospect, at age 79, maybe not the best of ideas.)

I jumped into my car and followed the truck like this was going to be a geriatric "Cannonball Run" People often say there's never a cop around when you need one, however, I was in luck, though it wasn't exactly a cop. As I was racing after the truck, a park ranger in a pick-up, came alongside me. I shouted that the truck up ahead had just side-swiped my car.

He swung right into action and joined the chase. With his lights flashing, he brought the driver to a halt on Pico, alongside Santa Monica High School. I stopped but the ranger ordered me to remain in my car saying he would handle it from here on in. (Smart move.)

Just then two cop cars pulled up. One of the cops joined the ranger and walked over to the driver of the truck where he asked for his driver's license. Then one of the cops came over to me and asked if I wanted to press charges.

"No," I replied, "I just want to collect for the damage to my car." The first cop told me that his driver's license didn't permit him to be driving trucks, only passenger cars. Therefore, a report was made. The police handed me a copy and we all left the scene.

Naturally, I reported the incident to the insurance company and they told me where to go to have the car repaired. However, I still continued parking on the street as I didn't have much choice. And wouldn't you know, about two weeks later, my car was hit again. This was getting like a bad TV re-run.

This time, I was informed of the accident by a neighbor who was awakened by the noise just below her window. It seems a teenager, riding a motorcycle, crashed into the rear of my car at 2:30 A.M. and, thank God, didn't hurt himself too badly.

When I saw the car the next morning, there was a police report under the windshield wiper. It's as if lightning had struck twice. Actually three times as, before I had a chance to bring the car in for repair, a bus driver sheared off the mirror on the driver's side of my car. It's like my car was target practice for careless drivers.

This driver, at least, was pleasant and eventually the City of Santa Monica paid for the damage. Some guy in my building told me to get rid of the car. He thought it was jinxed. It certainly felt like it.

Ouch! (And there were two others boo-boos.)

Six months later, when I was finally given a parking spot in the garage of my building, I purchased a 2004 Toyota Camry and was relieved to have my vehicle "off the street." It felt like I had been spending more time in auto body repair shops and insurance companies than enjoying life.

CHAPTER 86

WHAT A MAN WILL DO FOR LOVE (2004)

Years ago, I was introduced by a mutual friend to a very attractive woman named Vivian. She was also highly intelligent and well educated. I still remember our first date because something unusual happened the following day.

I went to my car in the early afternoon, got in, and noticed that Vivian had left her sunglasses on the passenger's seat. On close examination, they looked like prescription sunglasses, so I thought I'd call her as soon as I got back to my apartment. Exiting the car, I put her glasses in my shirt pocket because it was so hot I wasn't wearing a jacket.

I had a quarter to put into the parking meter but it slipped out of my hand and started to roll toward the sewer. In bending down to pick it up, Vivian's glasses slipped out of my pocket and fell into the sewer along with the quarter. Oh, brother.

What a stupid move. On closer inspection, I realized that at least there was no water in the sewer. I decided that first thing Monday morning I would go to City Hall and see if there was any way I could make arrangements to retrieve the glasses. It seemed a little far fetched but I was pretty desperate. (For the glasses, not the quarter!)

Bright and early on Monday morning, I went to City Hall. A little embarrassed, I explained to the receptionist what had happened. To my pleasant surprise, she asked me to describe the exact location, and I did.

After several calls and twenty minutes later she said I should go to the spot where the glasses had fallen and wait. "There will be a truck with two men in it. Flag them down and they will open the grate and get your glasses for you." Well, that's exactly what happened. I was delighted.

When the guy handed me the glasses, I was so grateful I took a ten-dollar bill from my wallet and said I wanted to treat each of them to a beer. "Oh, no," they said. "It's all part of the job." They refused to take any money.

They left and I went home, called Vivian and explained what had just happened. To my surprise, she laughed uproariously. When she caught her breath she explained why. First of all, they weren't her glasses, they were her daughter's. Secondly they weren't prescription but rather 99-cent store specials and her daughter probably had four others just like it. (At that point I was kinda glad the sanitation workers had turned down my $10.)

Vivian was very impressed with how persistent I had been. As I end this little tale, naturally, before I handed the glasses back to Vivian I had scrubbed them very thoroughly.

CHAPTER 87

THE PARKING VALET NEEDED LASIK
SURGERY (2005)

I try to go to South Florida every few years to visit my family, who, fortunately, also visit me here in Santa Monica. Sometimes I also use the Florida trip to go to New York to visit my cousin Jojo, of whom I'm very fond. Jojo's grandfather Jacob was my father's brother and her dad, Herbert was my 1st cousin who was 14 years older than I was. I was 12 when my dad passed and Herbert reached out to me in a "2nd father" way, for which I was forever grateful.

Extremely competent, Jojo was the office manager for a dentist in New York. A widow, she's the proud mother of three adult boys, one of whom is a NYPD officer, and seven grandchildren. She has a terrific boyfriend with whom she travels the world and she's also an avid tennis player. To my disappointment, on this trip, Jojo was going to be out of town so I stayed in Florida to help celebrate my first cousin Gertrude's 87 birthday. (Funny, now that I'm 98, 87 seems so young!)

I know this is a lot of "family" to follow, but Gertrude's father was my father's brother, so she and I are 1st cousins. Actually, I've called her Gert since we were kids. Anyway, given it was her birthday, I took her to the fanciest restaurant I could find. She was residing in a very pleasant "assisted living" facility but she needed a wheelchair because she had a bad knee and it was too painful to walk. Fortunately the restaurant had valet parking. (At least I thought it was fortunate.)

After a delicious dinner and a lot of wonderful "catching up" conversation, we left the restaurant. I casually handed my ticket to the attendant and continued chatting with Gert. The rental car was a dark gray Toyota Camry. After a while, I began to wonder why it was taking so long to bring the car around. I spotted the attendant but he said and with a critical tone, "I already brought it to you, sir."

I responded with my own critical tone, "If you already brought it to me, why would I still be standing here?" Well, obviously he hadn't brought me my car and the whole thing turned out to be a big mess, which I could title "How a great evening almost got ruined." (It still steams me when I think about what happened.)

What happened was a restaurant patron, who had probably had one drink too many, had driven away with my car by mistake after the valet, whose mind was who knows where, had given it to him. I don't know how the valet could get the cars confused, but then again, how did the customer drive off in someone else's car? In any event, finally the manager of the parking operation was called in and he went to work trying to sort things out.

The car that the customer had left behind was a dark gray Honda, so at least both cars had "dark gray" in common. In my car, I had some photographs my niece had given me, a sweater and a cap. And somehow the manager was able to track down what hotel this guy was registered at and left a message with the front desk explaining the whole fiasco.

Celebrating Cousin Gert's 87th birthday.

Now, all this took time. The sun had slowly disappeared, it was getting dark and Gert's back was aching pretty badly. Understandably, she just wanted to to return to her residence.

Straining not to lose my temper, I explained to the manager that I expected the situation to be rectified and pronto. My "suggestion" was that, until the mistake was untangled, they would have to drive Gert back to her place, only a ten-minute drive. But I also explained that I was staying in a hotel in Boca Rotan, fifty miles away and I insisted they drive me there asap. And that's what they did.

The next morning they returned my car, with everything intact, to my hotel. My car was driven by one driver, and another car followed behind so they would be able to get back.

I suppose all's well that ends well, but frankly the whole thing was a big pain in the ass, forgive my French. (I wonder if, when French people use profanity, do they say, "excuse my English?")

CHAPTER 88

SINGING FOR MY SUPPER (2005)

Vitello's is a very popular Italian restaurant in Studio City that serves delicious food. and used to be actor Robert Blake's favorite restaurant. That is, until his wife, Bonnie Lee Bakely, was murdered while sitting in their car parked in front.

Actually, as many may remember, Blake was accused of the 2001 murder of Bonnie Lee Bakely. (I suppose, by virtue of her marriage, she was Bonnie Lee Bakely Blake; try to say that fast three times.)

As you may recall, Blake spent 10 months in isolation in L.A. County Jail, until he finally was granted bail. In 2005, after a three-month criminal trial, Blake was found not guilty of the murder. Now, bear with me on this.

You know how I often seem to cross paths with famous or notable people. Well, Blake's defense attorney was Thomas Messereau Jr. And about twenty years ago I dated his mother Luisa Mesereau, who, among other things, confided in me that her son had been the heavyweight boxing champion of Harvard University and his father had been Superintendent of West Point! (All that, and 50 cents will get you a ride on the bus.)

Back to the Blake murder trial, after he was found not guilty, Bakely's children filed and won a civil suit against Blake for wrongful death and were awarded $30,000,000. Reportedly, in 2013, Blake settled the case with each of Bakely's four children receiving $500,000.

In any event, and though it seems ludicrous now, Blake was such a good customer at Vitello's they named an entree after him, "The Robert Blake Special," spinach in a tomato sauce served over pasta. (Sounds more like a Popeye Special than a Blake Special.)

I mention Vitello's because my friend, Hal Teich, frequently ate there with his lady friend, Muriel. My friendship with Hal goes back to WW2 when we both were machinists in Pearl Harbor during WW2. Anyway, Hal told me that on "amateur nights" Vitello patrons hand their sheet music to the pianist and entertain the customers. (Or bomb, depending on their talent.)

"Jerry," he said, "next Saturday night I want you to be our guest for dinner at Vitello's. Bring some sheet music and you will be called upon to sing." So it was, after we finished eating, the singing started.

The first singer was a middle-aged gentleman, who had an operatic voice. In Italian, mind you, he sang so beautifully, I remember thinking, "This man is professional quality talent." I started to have second thoughts about what I was getting myself into.

The next singer, a man about fifty, handed the pianist his music and sang a beautiful love song in an excellent voice and also sounded like a real pro. And, he like the first singer, received a very enthusiastic round of applause. By this time, I was thinking, "I'm way out of my league."

The singer who followed was a woman, about thirty-five, who sang songs from The Sound of Music and even reminded me a lot like Julie Andrews. Again, lots of applause. Now, it was my turn. I must admit that I went up with much trepidation. As I handed the sheet music to the piano player, I noticed some 8x10 glossies hanging in frames on the wall over the piano.

On closer inspection, I recognized the two men who sang before I did. As I had suspected, these two guys were part of the regular entertainment. Undaunted, well, almost, As I proceeded to sing "Impossible Dream" from Man of La Mancha. The applause was just as enthusiastic for me as for the performers before me. Naturally, I was encouraged to do another song.

In round two, the opera singer sang an aria from a German opera and in German! Big applause. The next singer performed another love song beautifully. Lots of applause when he finished. The woman was also very well received. I was next and sang, "New York, New York." Big hand, lots of applause. Now, I'm getting my confidence back.

In "round three," I sang Frank Sinatra's "My Way" and I got a big hand. In fact, some people came over to my table to tell me that I was the best singer.

I asked, "How could that be? The two men are professional singers. I'm not remotely in their league." One woman replied, "They have good voices but the opera singer sang in a foreign language, the other man sang songs we had never heard before, and the woman was kinda boring. You sang just as well and they were songs that we know and love."

One of these days I'm going to double date with Hal and Muriel and return to Vitello's. Wouldn't it be a blast if I ran into the same threesome? The question is, do they still serve the Robert Blake Special? (While editing this memoir, I called Vitello's and the answer was a definitive "no!" Ouch.)

CHAPTER 89

MY DELIGHTFUL DEBUT IN DOO-WOP (2007)

January 2007, I boarded the new Queen Mary II at Port Everglades in Fort Lauderdale, Florida. I signed up for a 26-day cruise, which was part of the maiden voyage of an 81-day world cruise. The ship was huge and each day I would explore, finding out where everything was. The second night, I found the grand lobby. Believe me, folks, it's aptly named. It really is a grand lobby. The grandest I've ever seen.

When I found it there was a group of four African-American Doo-Wop singers entertaining the passengers. The group's name was "Spank" and they would later explain that Doo-Wop goes back to the 1940's, popular in major cities. What makes it unique is, generally, there's no musical accompaniment at all. They clap their hands and snap their fingers and harmoniz beautifully.

I enjoyed their singing very much and was glad to hear that they were part of the ship's entertainment. I stayed until they finished and heard the lead singer announce that they would be back in the lobby at 10:30 P.M. to do their late show. I had dinner, saw the live entertainment in the showroom, and headed to the lobby to catch "Spank."

The next day, I was in the cafeteria during lunchtime. I had a tray full of food and was looking for a place to sit. It was the height of the lunch rush hour and every table was occupied. Just then, two members of Spank invited me to sit with them. I gladly accepted.

After getting acquainted, one of them asked where I was from. "New York, originally, having lived there for forty-one years, but now I reside in Los Angeles." "We're from New York!" one of the singers replied and then they both started to sing, "New York, New York."

As you know well by now, I do some singing, too, so when they began singing "New York, New York" I joined in. They stopped singing and I continued until the end of the song.

"Hey!" one of them said to the others, "This guy's got a good voice." Then he said to me, "How 'bout singing 'New York, New York' tonight with us in the lobby?" I looked at them in disbelief. "You really want me to sing with your harmony?" "Yes, that's exactly what we mean."

Well, as I always say you don't have to ask me twice when it comes to a slice of chocolate cake or singing in front of an audience. (Or any combination of the two.) So I gladly agreed to be there.

That night, when they were singing, there were about seventy-five people in the lobby. Finally, when they were winding down their act they called on me to perform. They gave me a nice intro and announced that I was going to sing "New York, New York."

I sang and evidently the passengers liked what they heard because I received a big hand. As soon as I got through the lead singer asked, "Can you come back tomorrow night with another song?"

An old Jew and 4 African-Americans.

So, the next night I sang "Impossible Dream" from "Man of La Mancha." This time, the lobby was standing room only. Can you guess what happened next? Another invitation to come back a third night.

Each night, the lobby was getting bigger crowds. Word had gotten around the ship that one of the passengers, albeit rather elderly, had a good singing voice and was backed up by an extraordinarily talented group. No one back home would believe it. For that matter, I couldn't believe it.

This time I sang Frank Sinatra's "My Way." All I can say is at age 85, I've been fortunate enough to experience many wonderful, gratifying experiences in my life. I must confess, this was one of the finest days. (Although, to be technical, it was at night.)

CHAPTER 90

DYAN CANNON AND I "CHAT" ABOUT CARY (2011)

When I was 17, I saw Gunga Din, a 1939 RKO adventure film that was "set"in India (but filmed in the Sierra Nevada range.) It starred Cary Grant,Victor McLaglen and Douglas Fairbanks Jr and was loosely based on the poem of the same name by Rudyard Kipling. Largely because of Grant, the movie had a big impact on me and I wasn't alone. Grant would star, or have a major role, in 72 movies spanning an iconic 34-year career.

Never one to take himself too seriously, Grant was handsome, debonair and had a terrific sense of comic timing that explained his broad appeal. He became a legend in Hollywood's Golden Age. Every man wanted to be Cary Grant and every woman wanted to be with him. Grant said himself, "Everybody would like to be Cary Grant. So would I."

However, Grant started life with more than a few strikes against him. First, per-haps,was his name, Archibald Leach. (Doesn't exactly have the same ring as "Cary Grant," does it?)

He was born in 1904 in Horfield, Bistol, England. When he was 9, he was told that his mother had run off to the seaside. Soon afterwards, he was told that she was dead. Neither was true.

Reportedly, Grant's father, Elias, an alcoholic, had her committed to a lunatic asy-lum, so he could continue drinking and philandering. Some 20 years later, his father confessed to the deception and Grant visited his mother. In fact, he cared for her for the rest of her life, but the damage to both was sadly irreparable.

Grant was in many classic Hollywood movies, including 4 directed by Alfred Hitchcock (Suspicion, Notorious, To Catch a Thief, and North by Northwest.) One movie he turned down, however, was James Bond in Dr. No. At 58, Grant didn't think the role was right for him even though Ian Flemming, who created the character, said that the basis for the classic spy was none other than Grant himself.

In his personal life, Grant would marry 5 times. His 4th wife, Dyan Cannon, was one of my favorite light comedy actresses. She was 28 when they married, he was 61. They had one child, Jennifer, now 53.

About eight days ago I read that Dyan was coming to our Main Library to talk about her recent book, "Dear Cary, My Life with Cary Grant." I decided to go but during the day I had to be downtown for jury duty. Some might think it old fashioned, but I wore my best black blazer with coordinating shirt, slacks and tie for the occasion. I mention it because I think it might have been a factor later in the evening.

When I arrived at the library after dinner and still in my blazer, the Martin Luther King Auditorium was packed. Luckily, I spotted a seat in the 3rd row directly in Dyan Cannon's line of vision. I listened attentively as she was interviewed by a newspaper reporter and then it was time for the question and answer period.

Immodest as it may sound, I felt like Dyan Cannon's eyes were often on me, or so it seemed. I assumed it might have been because I was the only man in the audience of 125 who was dressed up, so to speak.

When the Q and A period began, Dyan answered questions posed by a few women and then I raised my hand. When she called on me I stood up and said, "The men's clothing industry owes Cary Grant a very big vote of thanks because in every one of his movies he always looked so well-groomed. His taste in clothes was always impeccable and whatever he wore fit so well."

Dyan's answer took me and the entire room by surprise. "Jerry you're absolutely right, Cary looked wonderful in clothes, but between you and me, he looked even better without clothes." It took a full minute for the laughter to subside.

I decided I had to buy Dyan's book and stood in line waiting for her to write something on the inside cover. When my turn came, Dyan looked up at me and said into the microphone, "Here comes handsome Jerry." I was almost 90 so, trust me, she was just being kind. On the other hand, having been married to Cary Grant, she was something of an expert on "handsome."

CHAPTER 91

IS 98 TOO LATE FOR ME IN ADVERTISING? (2012)

In 2012, I was talking on the phone with my nephew Mark, my late brother Arthur's only son, who lives in Jacksonville, Florida. And since it had been a while, he invited me for a visit. "There's always a room for you here, Uncle Jerry," he said. So I decided to take him up on his kind offer. After our chat, I phoned Super Shuttle to see if they operated in Jacksonville.

Sure enough, Super Shuttle does operate out of Jacksonville. This was important to me because then they could pick me up at the airport and take me to my nephew's house. You could ask why wouldn't I have him pick me up? The answer is because he's a busy lawyer and I don't like to be a burden.

The man at Super Shuttle, named Joe, observed, "I see in the computer, Mr. Rosenblum, that you live on 5th in Santa Monica." "Why yes," I responded, "why do you ask?" "I used to live in Santa Monica ages ago. I worked for my father who owned the Midas Muffler shop on Colorado and 5th, a half a block from where you live."

I couldn't believe my ears and I'll explain why. In 1987 my car was stolen in Santa Monica from my building's underground garage and was later found in a parking lot on Colorado and 6th Street. And when the police called to tell me they found my car, they said it was from a tip from a young man who worked at the Midas Muffler shop. He happened to park his motorcycle next to my car every night and every night it got more and more stripped.

Joe interrupted me, exclaiming excitedly, "That was me!" Now I was completely stunned. Out of 330 million people in the U.S. what are the odds that I would be talking to the one person who reported my car stolen?

Suddenly I felt like I was talking to an old friend and he felt the same. He explained he now lived in Phoenix but that he still missed Santa Monica. So I said, "If you ever visit here, you'll have to let me buy you lunch. Do you like deli food?" In fact he did. And we agreed I'm going to take him to Fromin's, my treat.

With some sadness, I explained that Midas was no longer there. It's now a Marriott Hotel, across the street from the Metro. It's all part of the modernization of Santa Monica about which I have mixed feelings.

I thoroughly enjoyed chatting with Joe and and I can report that the Super Shuttle service in Jacksonville was great. And of course my visit with my nephew was wonderful as always.

This story, now that I think about it, has a bit of a "full circle" to it. The only thing that could tie a ribbon around this tale is if Joe comes to town and we go to Fromin's. (Now, I'm wondering if I can get an endorsement from Fromin's?)

Actually, by my count, I've inadvertently given "free publicity" to Midas Muffler, Super Shuttle, Marriott Hotel and Fromin's. At 98, is it too late for me in advertising?

CHAPTER 92

"YOU'RE IN LUCK, THERE'S ONE TICKET LEFT" (2014)

This story deals with my grand-nephew, Adam Roberts, and his husband, Craig Johnson. Adam has a law degree from Emory University, primarily because his parents wanted him to have a profession to fall back on in the event his writing career didn't pan out. Suffice it to say, his writing career has definitely panned in! He's written two best-selling cookbooks and just recently sold a screenplay to Netflix.

Craig is also a writer and a director whose latest movie at the time of this writing is Wilson starring Woody Harrelson and Laura Dern. The movie before that was titled Skeleton Twins and premiered two years ago. One day back then I read that the movie was opening in the Landmark Theater Complex fairly near me so I decided to go to the premier. The ad stated that after the movie the actors and the director would stay for a Q & A. session.

That night I drove to the theater, parked my car, took the elevator and then the escalator up to the theater level, and asked for a ticket for Skeleton Twins. The young lady said, "You're in luck, there's one ticket left. Second row center." Luck? I'd be right up against the screen. "Sorry," she said, "it's a sellout."

But then I thought that when the actors and the director come out on stage Craig would be able to see "Uncle Jerry." It took about ten minutes to adjust my eyes because I was sitting so close to the screen I thought my neck was going to fall off. But, after ten minutes or so, I got used to it. (Besides, I have an excellent chiropractor.)

I thoroughly enjoyed the movie and, immediately afterwards chairs were brought on stage. Craig sat exactly in my line of vision, about twelve feet from where I was sitting.

He asked the audience of two hundred how they liked the movie? Lots of applause. Craig didn't see me at first because he had to get used to the bright lights. Then suddenly he saw me. "Uncle Jerry!" he shouted out. Then he pointed to me and said to the audience, "This man is 92-years-old." The audience gave me a nice round of applause, I suppose just for living this long.

About fifteen minutes later after the question and answer period was almost over, the M.C. asked me how I liked the movie and suddenly the attention was on me. "It's true. I am 92 and I've seen a great many movies. I love this one because it breaks new ground. I predict it will have a long run and take in lots of money at the box office."

Again, a big round of applause. The M.C. at that point decided to end the proceedings on a high note. The people on stage thanked the audience and left the stage. Craig waved goodbye to me and as I was exiting two complete strangers shook my hand, again I guess because I was 92.

As I got closer to the lobby another gentleman stopped me. He said his name was Peter and that he had gone to high school with my nephew, Mark. They both attended Valley Stream High School on Long Island in New York.

Mark is a very prominent criminal defense attorney in Jacksonville, Florida.

When Craig shouted out "Uncle Jerry," Peter remembered he had heard my nephew Mark speak about his Uncle Jerry. He put two and two together and figured I was "the" Uncle Jerry. He said he was glad he finally got to meet me. It made me feel terrific and was the end to a great evening.

All in all, the young lady who sold me my ticket to the movie was 100% right. It turned out I was definitely in luck.

CHAPTER 93

MY NERVOUS RETURN TO THEATER PALISADES (2014)

One day in my Emeritus "singing instruction" class, Elizabeth Edwards, a honcho (or, should I say, a "honchette?") at the Theater Palisades, visited us and said she was looking for amateur senior talent for an upcoming revue. She picked me and seven other senior singers for the production.

I was a little self-conscious, because, in 2004 I had auditioned for a part for the Theater Palisades production of "Pajama Game." At 80 and with no real theatrical experience, I only auditioned for the experience of it and was totally surprised when they offered me the role.

I was also embarrassed. You see I had a luxury cruise vacation booked in 3 weeks so I apologized profusely. Inasmuch as this "faux pas" had been so long ago, I hoped nobody would remember.

Theater Palisades is a wonderful little venue. The rehearsals went very well. They allotted me two songs and on the night of the big show, I performed "If I were a Rich Man," fast becoming my signature song and "Before the Parade Passes By" from the show "Hello Dolly."

A good friend lent me a pair of boots that Tevya might have worn and a tallis (Jewish prayer shawl.) I already had a black Greek fisherman's hat, so if nothing else I looked the part. Apparently I also "sang the part," because I got a rousing ovation from both numbers.

I was a rich man ... for one night.

Thankfully, as ten years had passed, no one on the Theater staff remembered I had kinda stiffed them almost a decade earlier. (Actually, now that I think about it, I hope none of them is reading this. Oops.)

CHAPTER 94

A FRIENDSHIP FOR THE AGES (2015)

If you think someone in their 90's can't make a new friendship with someone in their 20's, that rivals any they've had in their lifetime, think again. That said, it was a complete surprise.

I happen to live in a wonderful multi-story seniors only apartment building in Santa Monica. It's owned by the Salvation Army and is run beautifully. It's not at all uncommon that we get volunteers from the outside to help us with various activities. One day in March, 2015 was such a fortunate day.

Katie Miller, 24 at the time, worked in marketing in an office down the street. Attractive, bright and resourceful, she's now a Senior Marketing Executive who travels the world. But in the days I'm referring to she evidently had some spare time and an inner need to help seniors.

As she would later explain, her grandfather on her dad's side, lives in Florida and her grandparents on her mom's side, live in Connecticut, all of whom Katie missed dearly. She thought she might enjoy connecting with seniors locally and maybe helping them with computer and cell phone problems. Believe it or not, we have quite a few seniors who have those devices and were in dire need of assistance. So, for some, Katie's visit was like a gift from above. (Or the nearest Apple Store.)

When Katie approached me, I jokingly responded, "You've got the wrong guy, young lady, I don't go near those contraptions." Katie joked back. "I'm not religious about computers, so I don't want to convert you."

I was curious what motivated Katie kindness and generosity. Fortunately, she accepted my offer to buy her coffee and a pastry at a nearby restaurant when she was done with her tutoring.

So began the most wonderful friendship in my life. And people seem to love our unique bonding, two people over 70 years apart in age. In fact, a newspaper story was written about about us and it went all over the Internet.

As Katie faced serious career decisions, she appreciated my experience, objective listening and occasional advice. She often would frequently invite me to holiday parties at her work where I met dozens of her fellow-employees. And, for my 95th birthday, she threw me a surprise party at a Karaoke Club where I sang for her and her friends and many of my older friends.

When Katie would go on lengthy business trips, to Europe, for example, she would send me dozens of post cards. She had given me her itinerary so, for my part, I'd send her post cards in advance so she'd hear the news from home upon her arrival at the various cities.

My BFF, Katie Miller.

Upon Katie's return, I threw her a surprise "Welcome Home" party at a fancy restaurant attended by 15 of her friends. Again, not to be immodest, but I seemed to be adopted by many of her friends as their surrogate grandfather. (When in fact, I'm really old enough to be their great-grandfather.)

Often we'd go for lunch and chat. Other days we'd go for a walk in the park taking her "wonder dog" Teddy. Then Katie asked if she could make an Instagram page for me so I might be a surrogate grandparent for millennials. Somehow I have 21,200 Instagram followers. (Actually the "how" is all Katie.)

With her I-phone, Katie has recorded 14 videos of me singing and has put them on YouTube and Instagram. As a result, on my birthday, I've gotten hundreds of "snail mail" birthday cards from all over the world. I've even gotten many gifts, among the most unusual, being 2 gallons of gourmet ice cream packed in dry ice.

It was from an Instagram friend at the University of Pennsylvania, where apparently they make ice cream. If they don't already, they oughta market it, because, for me, it was the best tasting ice cream ever. Ben and Jerry, look out.

Katie is in charge of my Instagram page where we often get questions from followers on various subjects, including my diet and exercise regimen and my keys to a long and full life. Katie records my answers and posts them back on Instagram, which is gratifying to me and seemingly rather popular among my new friends.

As I wrote in my first chapter, one of my earliest "follower"was Congresswoman Alexandria Ocasio-Cortez. If and when I go on a book tour I'm hoping to go to NYC and maybe she'll introduce me at a book signing in her district. (My fingers are crossed, which might explain any typos.)

Meanwhile, as Katie's executive career continues to grow, I gently encourage her to find the right boyfriend she could marry one day. I tell her, "There's a lucky guy out there who doesn't even know it because he hasn't met you yet."

I gather, as many in her age and career, Katie doesn't have much time for relationships. I confess one day I very much want to sing at her wedding. Apparently, at this late stage in my life, I've turned into a Jewish mother.

CHAPTER 95

MY HILARY CLINTON "AFFAIR" (2015)

I've been following Hilary Clinton's career since she was the First Lady of Arkansas and then the First Lady of the U.S. I remember Bill saying Hilary would have made a better president than he was. Given her intelligence, experience he made a very persuasive case.

In the past, I had enjoyed Hilary's autobiography Living History. On June 19, 2015, to be exact, I noticed an ad in the L.A. Times that Hilary was going to do a book signing for her latest tome, Hard Choices at the Barnes & Noble Book Store in The Grove, a big shopping center in L.A.

The funny thing is that, about a month earlier and seemingly out of nowhere, I had awoken one morning with the tune "That's Entertainment" going on and on in my brain. Especially since my retirement, I've been a bit of an amateur song writer. So I decided that I should put my own words to the melody and write a campaign song for Hilary.

In two hours I had the whole song finished. A friend of mine is a professional pianist and has a recording studio nearby. Expertly, he transferred my singing of the Hilary campaign song to a compact disc.

So when I saw the ad about the book signing I thought I would buy the book, have Hilary sign it, and at the same time give her the compact disc. I planned on going early because, if I didn't, I'd end up behind a mob of people in front of me.

So that morning I arrived at the shopping center at 7 A.M. I parked my car and proceeded to walk to the book store. It was very quiet at that early morning hour.

Just then I saw a security guard pointing me to go to the rear of the Barnes & Noble book store. When I got there I couldn't believe ,my eyes. There were hundreds of people standing in line or, in other words, even at 7 A.M. I was going to be behind a mob of people in front of me.

I thought to myself, "Jerry, what are you getting into? You're 93. Are you going to stand out here in the hot sun? Who knows how long it will take until you actually get into the book store." (Just for the record,when I talk to myself like that, at least I don't do it out loud.)

The weather forecasters had predicted it would be hot that day. If anything, they understated it. Then I thought, "What the heck, I'm here already. I'll just remain in line and by 9 A.M. it's bound to move." I thought wrong.

As I continued to debate whether to stay in line or not, more people were coming and standing behind me. So it was, I struck up conversation with two young ladies. As I looked at the crowd I realized I was clearly the oldest person in line. (For that matter, I might have been the oldest person in the zip code.)

I kid you not, we stood there for two hours without moving. Not an inch. As you know by now, I love to tell stories and I had killed some time that way but, after 90 minutes, I had basically long run out of my "A material" and was "working" what sounded more like a vaudeville act in chatting with my new-found friends in line. In the meantime, I needed to avail myself of a men's room. And pronto.

Fortunately, one of the young ladies said politely, "Jerry, go, we'll save your place." But, when I got back, I was shocked. My "place" was gone! The group had gone into the book store. Talk about bad timing!

I called a security guard over and explained to her what had just happened. After a few exasperating moments, she finally took sympathy on me, "You wait right here. I'll have another security guard escort you into the store." Which is exactly what happened.

And I was delighted to see my two female friends. In fact, one of them rushed up. "Jerry we bought you a copy," and handed me a shopping bag that contained Hilary's book. I reached t for my wallet to pay them back but they refused to take the money. Instead, they shared an expression I had never heard of.

"Pay it forward," one of the girls said. "Do someone else a favor." The book plus tax came to about thirty dollars. Even though I insisted they adamantly refused to take my money and they said goodbye. The only problem was, I wanted the book signed by Hilary. For that, believe it or not, there was...ready? ANOTHER LINE!

Now we were directed outside the mall where people were lined up in front of a restaurant. Just then a waitress, who had seen me through the window, came out and asked if I would like a chair.

She was so sweet. She not only brought out a chair but she handed me a ten dollar gift certificate for the restaurant. Now I was sitting on a chair and it felt so good you can't imagine.(When you're 93, you will.)

Just then I noticed a middle-aged woman standing about six people in front of me on crutches. I remembered "pay it forward," so I walked over and told her we could share the chair. She was thrilled.

Finally, after standing a total of six very long hours, we were directed to the second floor via an escalator. Hilary was on the third floor and I could see her about thirty feet away signing books. I took out the compact disc which was in an envelope.

Just then a burly female secret service officer asked me rather gruffly, "What's in the envelope?" I told her I wrote a campaign song for Hilary. "Give it to me," she said forcefully, "and I'll make sure she gets it." What was I going to say?

A few minutes later I was standing directly in front of Hilary Clinton. Finally! Thoroughly exhausted from over 6 hours of waiting, I joked, "You know, Madam Secretary, I was a young man when I first got on line!"

Hilary burst out laughing, which, honestly, made the wait worthwhile. We chatted briefly and then she graciously signed my book. At the time I didn't know if the secret service woman gave her the disc or not. I still don't know. But she did get to hear it and I'll explain how I know.

Katie had recorded my singing the song and posted it on Instagram and YouTube. Hilary either heard the song that way or maybe the Secret Service woman gave her the disc. Or maybe it was both. In any event, a few weeks later I received not one but two letters from Hilary thanking me for the song I wrote and for the contribution to her campaign. Both letters are in picture frames on my dresser.

Not to get all political on you, but have to admit I would never write a song about Donald Trump. In a way it's too bad because I already have the title in mind "The Lyin' King."

CHAPTER 96

THOMAS WOLFE WAS WRONG (2018)

In the summer of 2018, and at age 96, I had a nostalgic urge to visit New York City, the town where I was born and raised and where I lived for the first 41 years of my life. Since I was going all alone, my friends were concerned, especially Katie. The truth is, while I felt confident I could handle the trip now, in a few years, who knew.

Of course I didn't dare tell Katie for fear of worrying her. Instead, I assured her I would be fine and promised I'd call at least once a day and she said she'd do the same. Little did I know how much I would need one of her calls.

For 5 days I was to stay at the the Hotel New Yorker on 8th Avenue and W. 34th because it's midtown Manhattan location was ideal for the places I wanted to visit, Plus it's easy to get a cab anytime at that hotel because they come and go constantly. So even though Thomas Wolfe titled his novel "You Can't Go Home Again," that's exactly what I did.

On my first day, I thought I'd ease into it. But soon, I could tell the city was either much faster than I remembered or I was much slower. Since I had loved Broadway musicals, even as a child, I walked slowly down the Great White Way and "window shopped." Unfortunately, none of the productions were anything I desperately wanted to see and, the few that I might, were sold out for the next 10 years and, somehow, I don't think I'll be coming back in 2028, though I'm not ruling it out. Still, I loved walking and looking like a Broadway groupie.

I stopped for lunch at the old Carnegie Deli and it seemed almost exactly the same, except the sandwiches were even bigger than I recalled. I had corned beef on rye, a bowl of cole slaw and extra pickles. I could barely finish half of the giant portions so I had them give me a doggie bag.

Apparently this first day took more energy than I thought, because I suddenly got very fatigued but in a pleasant "sight-seeing" way. I decided it was time to walk back to my hotel room.

When I lay down on the bed I started to think maybe Katie had been right. Maybe I had bitten off more than I could chew. After all, I wasn't 92 anymore.(Work with me folks, that may be my best joke so far!)

I sort of dreaded calling Katie but she beat me to it. She knows me so well she could tell by the sound of my voice I wasn't 100%. Actually that's why she was calling but this just reinforced it. Albeit diplomatically, Katie let me know there were going to have to be some changes in my comings and goings on this trip. She can be strict, trust me.

"I've taken care of everything, Jerry. Tomorrow, a college friend of mine who's taking the day off work, will pick you up in front of your hotel at 1 pm. His name is Doug Strauss and he's an assistant D.A. He's going to be your chauffeur for part of the day and for the other part, you're going to get a very special set of chauffeurs. So no more stairs, long walks, subways and cabs. Got it?" "Yes, Sergeant, loud and clear."

Has anyone called my lawyer?

At 1 pm sharp the following afternoon, I was standing in front of my hotel and Doug was right on time. What a mensch as he couldn't have been nicer. He drove me on the Westside Highway all the way to Coney Island where, to my surprise, we pulled into a police station. Two young cops were standing by their squad car waiting for us. I joked to Doug, "Did I forget to pay a parking ticket in 1962?"

Doug told me the officers were going to drive us to my old neighborhood and, after all that he would drive me back to the hotel. He introduced me to the police officers and then he and I got in the back seat as the police drove us all the way to Brighton Beach.

They asked directions to the street I grew up on and as we slowly drove by so many memories from almost 90 years flooded into my brain. I saw the old playground in back of P.S. 225 where I used to play basketball and was amazed the baskets were still there. It's was as though time had magically stood still. Our next stop was my high school, James Madison, which was nearby.

FYI, Madison has some pretty famous alumni, given that 7 of them have won a Nobel Prize! (I wasn't even nominated.) Illustrious alumni include Senators Bernie Sanders, and Chuck Schumer, and former Senator Senator Norm Coleman and Supreme Court Justice Ruth Bader Ginsburg who was...ready for this? A baton twirler at Madison High.

The list goes on! Famed singer, songwriter, composer, pianist and environmental activist, Carole King, widely recognized as the best female songwriter of the latter half of the 20th century, graduated from Madison. "Judge Judy" (Judy Sheindlin), actor Martin Landau and billionaire businessman, Lawrence Tisch, a friend of mine in high school, all Madison grads! (Depending on your definition of "illustrious," comedian Andrew Dice Clay graduated from Madison as well.)

Lastly, if I wanted to feel old, which I don't particularly, I graduated Madison two years before Bernie Sanders was born! Meanwhile, I'm told some Madison alumni are checking to see if I, Jerry from Brighton Beach, might be the oldest living graduate. (This, even though I was was never a baton twirler or Nobel Prize winner.)

We then drove to the apartment building where I lived from from 6 until I was 10. And amazingly, the building was still there. And even more amazingly, it looked exactly the same. As I stared, I half expected Rod Serling to suddenly appear and say, "Is it like you never left, Jerry?"

Later, to my surprise and delight, the police drove their car onto the Brighton Beach boardwalk at about 5 miles an hour. As we headed for Coney Island, on the left side was the Atlantic Ocean and the beach. On the right side was the amusement park with all the rides.

Waving at me, passersby looked into the police car trying to figure who was this old man and why was he smiling from ear to ear. Some, I assumed, might have thought I was famous. Others, more likely, might have thought I'd been arrested and my lawyer was sitting next to me. I just smiled back and waved. I felt like the Grand Marshall in a parade.

From Brighton Beach we drove to Flatbush and down Avenue U where I saw Mr. Weiner's drugstore where I worked all through high school. Across the street was the candy store where I bought "egg cream sodas" on a hot summer day. I could almost relive how refreshing those sodas were. I also used to buy the delicious Mellow Rolls, which were ice cream and cake in a Dixie cup. (As I look back, how did I <u>not</u> get fat?)

With my very special "magical mystery tour" coming to an end, we drove back to the police station. I thanked the police profusely and they said how much they had enjoyed themselves, too. Then Doug drove me back to my hotel and thanked me for including him in going down my memory lane. What a guy.

And what a magnificent day that turned out to be and all due to my friend Katie. Before I drifted off to sleep that night, I replayed all the wonderful memories of my childhood that I had been so lucky to re-live. However, I couldn't stop wondering if any of those passersby on the Coney Island boardwalk went home that evening and told their family, "I think I just saw the oldest criminal in history."

CHAPTER 97

LITTLE MISS SUNSHINE IS ALL GROWN UP (2019)

In January, I celebrated my 98th birthday with a party given to me by my friends, and, to quote some of the younger ones, "it was a major blast." One unexpected "plus" to my getting older is that each year my birthday party seems somehow better than the one before.

This year's celebration was at a Karaoke bar in Culver City and the place was packed. Attending the party were long term friends and friends whom I've met over recent years, through Katie and her bright co-workers. All of that, AND I got to sing my heart out on stage to a very appreciative audience made it the best birthday of them all. (That is, until next year?)

The group seemed to love celebrating my birthday as they might their grandfather's. So I was the beneficiary of all that love and they seemed so happy to be able to share it. Am I lucky or what?

One of the young women, Abigail, whom I didn't know, came to the party with my friend Dana, who introduced us. As we chatted, Abigail kept affectionately calling me the "birthday boy." I haven't been a "boy" in so long, trust me, I loved every minute.

At one point I asked Abigail if she were in school or did she work or was she independently wealthy and lived in a mansion. (If it was the latter, I added, "Might you have need for an elderly but well-mannered butler who loves to sing?")

She laughed and said she was an actress and no she wasn't independently wealthy. I'm a huge fan of movies and immediately inquired if she had ever been in any film I might have seen.

Abigail paused a moment and asked if I had ever seen "Little Miss Sunshine." OMG, as they say on the Internet. I suddenly realized I was talking to Abigail Breslin, who, at 9, not only starred in that hit movie, but received an Academy Award Nomination!

I didn't want to embarrass her, but I was highly impressed. And the funny thing is, she is still very much like the outgoing, smart and strong willed girl in the movie, only now she's all grown up. As we chatted, her boyfriend, Ira, joined us and soon someone took a photo of the three of us.

As Ira left momentarily to get us drinks, Abbie (as she asked me to call her) insisted on taking me to lunch very soon to celebrate my birthday just the three of us, including Ira. Honestly, I thought she was just being polite but a week later she called and we made a date for lunch. Again, she insisted it was her treat.

So it was, two weeks later we had lunch at the upscale Hilstone Restaurant on 2nd Street and Wilshire. Abbie handed me a present, the framed photo of her, me and Ira. (Which sits on my mantle as I write this now.)

As we ate we talked about a variety of subjects, but given my love of movies, I steered some of the conversation toward her career. In fact, for many years I've taken a film review class at Emeritus College for seniors in Santa Monica and I asked if she might consider talking to the students.

To my delight, she said she'd be honored and she'd even bring a high definition copy of the movie to our class, if our professor, Dr. Sheila Laffey, might like that. (Sheila, who is beloved by the class, was over the moon as we'd never had an Oscar-nominated performer bring a movie and be open to questions and answers.)

The class took place on April 17th. But a few hours earlier, I took Abbie and Aaron and Dr. Laffey out to lunch. It was in honor of the occasion and also as a belated birthday celebration for Abbie who turned 23 on the 14th. (23? I have ties older than that!)

After lunch we went directly to class and the room was SRO. As planned, as soon as I introduced Abbie the entire class burst out singing, "Happy Birthday, Dear Abbie." It totally caught her off guard and I could tell she was touched.

The movie was terrific (what a cast) and the Q & A was extremely interesting. It was fascinating to get an "inside" view. I think Abbie was 9 when she appeared in "Little Miss Sunshine." She's so talented, here's what IMDB says about her, "Her unique and charismatic talents have contributed to her versatile roles in both comedy and drama." Not bad, huh?

Suffice it to say, Abbie's "appearance" was a huge success. Afterwards, everyone patted me on the back like I was now a big time movie producer who had delivered a movie star to our little class. One classmate joked, "Do you think you can get us Lady Gaga?"

Actually, the joke is getting a little old as each week he asks me how I'm progressing with Gaga. Who knows, maybe I'll call her agent. A big advantage of being 98 is you're long passed being embarrassed anymore,which, I must confess, is liberating.

Oscar-nominated actress and my friend, Abigail Breslin.

P.S.: As I write this, Abigail has just returned from France where she filmed Stillwater, a movie she co-stars with Matt Damon. A la the Amanda Knox story, Abigail plays an American student studying abroad who is accused of a murder she didn't commit and Damon plays her estranged father who sacrifices everything to free her. Abigail insists I be her "date" at the movie's premier. I can hardly wait!

CHAPTER 98

DID I FINALLY MEET MY GUARDIAN ANGEL? (2019)

Despite the title of this memoir, I don't actually believe that angels from heaven protect humans on earth, or, in my case, a young boy of 12 who just lost his father. Then again, I can't actually say that angels don't do just that. After you read this last chapter, I'll leave it to you to decide.

As this chaper begins, I was on my way to visit my friend, Hal Teich, whom I first met when we both were machinists in Pearl Harbor during WWII. Keep in mind, that was a mere 76 years ago.

Hal and I have remained in close touch all these years as he lives nearby in Brentwood, an upscale section of Los Angeles. Normally we'd meet for lunch at the Soup Plantation on San Vincente as it's halfway between both of us. But Hal wanted to show me his house that I'd never seen in the over 50 years years hes' lived there, so I agreed to drive there. Let's just say it was a "memorable" drive, as in a memory you'd like to forget.

First of all it was at night, which, even at 98, is generally is not a problem for me. In fact I joke that older women are attracted to me, not because I'm a dapper dresser, or because I'm a good conversationalist, but because I still drive at night. Apparently, in the world of senior women, that's sexy.

The problem with this particular night drive was the street Hal lives on. Tigertail Road is way up in the hills, it was cold and windy, and the worst part, there were almost no lights on the street. Evidently the residents like it that way, as I suppose it gives a more rural feel to the neighborhood. Another problem was the large houses were set back far from the street so, from the car, I couldn't make out the addresses for the life of me.

I found myself grumbling and wishing we were meeting at the Soup Plantation. If Hal wanted me to see the inside of his house, he could send photos. Isn't that what the Internet is for? Of course I'm just joking as Hal, bless him, is a dear friend who was very proud of his what I've been told is a beautiful house.

I decided the only solution was to stop the car and go on foot to check a house address so I'd have an idea of how far or close I was to Hal's place. What I didn't realize is that the hill I parked on was far steeper than I imagined. Uh oh.

When I got out of my car, because of the steep grade, I lost my balance and fell backwards. I hit my head on the asphalt and wound up flat on my back, in the street. The cap I was wearing absorbed some of the blow, but I could feel a cut on my head though, thankfully, it didn't feel very deep. That said, I couldn't get up. Hard as I tried I just couldn't get up on my feet. It was rather alarming, to say the least.

I didn't have a cell phone and it would be pointless to yell as the houses were so far from the street no one would hear. Unfortunately, there wasn't a soul on the sidewalk. I thought maybe a car would come and the driver might help, but dark as it was, he or she could could just as easily run me over. In the wind and cold, I actually thought I might have to lie in the street until dawn and hopefully someone walking their dog, would find me. To be totally honest, it was a very grim situation I found myself in and I knew it.

After what seemed like fifteen minutes or so of just laying in the street, I heard a woman's voice and she sounded very alarmed. In the darkness, I vaguely saw a tall, athletic woman, with long hair blowing in the wind, I'm guessing in her early 30's, come out of the shadows hurrying toward me. "Are you all right, sir?" she asked.

I explained what had happened and wondered if she could call 911. Oddly enough, she didn't answer my question which added to my confusion. Instead, she asked if I thought with her help did I think I could stand. I doubted she would be strong enough to lift me up, but I was willing to try as lying in the street wasn't exactly like lying on a foam memory mattress.

As she knelt behind my bloody head, and put her hands under my shoulders, to my shock, she proceeded to seemingly lift me off the ground and back on my feet. The whole thing, the cold, the wind, my fall, her lifting me etc, was surreal, but I was up!

I leaned against the car, started to check myself out and was reassured as it felt like nothing was broken. Feeling significantly better just being upright, I turned to thank her. But shockingly, she was gone! She had seemingly disappeared as mysteriously as she had arrived.

I felt so disoriented by the events of the last twenty minutes, I actually thought for a second maybe I had imagined her. But no, absolutely not. I could even describe her voice and I vividly remember her perfume. But why would she just vanish?

And then the strangest thing happened. Perhaps it was just shock from what I had gone through, but tears rolled down my cheeks. Only it didn't feel like 98-year-old Jerry crying. No. It felt more like 12- year-old Jerome. It was though I had been holding the tears in for eight decades. I found myself remembering the very night when my dad had died and vividly picture the police officer gently telling my mother, "We tried but there was nothing we could do. I'm so sorry, ma'am but he's gone."

After a minute or more, I snapped out of my reverie. I wiped the tears from my face and breathed deeply. I felt I was okay enough to carefully walk to the house to see the actual address. I gingerly opened the car door and got the piece of paper on which I had written Hal's address.

Timidly, I walked the flower lined path that led to the front door. I was hoping that I wasn't far from Hal's because I didn't relish the thought of getting back into the car and driving in search of his place.

As I got the near the front door, my hand was shaking as I glanced at the crumpled paper to check Hal's address. As if the evening needed any more eerie aspects, guess what? I was at Hal's house! How was it that when I stopped I had been exactly at Hal's. I was too rattled to do any more thinking, so I just rang the doorbell. There was no answer and I hoped Hal hadn't fallen asleep as he was prone to do. But finally the light above the door came on which was a relief.

When Hal opened the door he went from happy to worried as he could see I was all disheveled. He was even more worried when I blurted out what had happened to. He immediately pulled me into the house and sat me down in a large leather chair in the living room. Upset by my cut, he raced to the bathroom he said to get a warm wash cloth. As he gently dabbed at the wound he reassured me thankfully the wound was relatively minor. (For once my being "hard headed" might have paid off.)

As Hal continued to attend to my wound, I described the young woman who had helped me to Hal. Having lived in the neighborhood over a half century, maybe he knew her so I could thank her. Puzzled, he said she didn't sound at all familiar.

I jokingly suggested that maybe she had been my guardian angel. "What are you talking about?" he asked thoroughly puzzled, not that I blamed him. "It's a long story, Hal, and we're both old enough as it is."

So, has there been an angel looking after me since I was 12 when my dad died? Or have I just imagined her these past 85 years? Either way, I've had a wonderful, rich life. I've been blessed in so many ways with family and friends, and even my Instagram friends who send me birthday cards. I've said this before, but they all have added years to my life and life to my years.

So we've come to the end of this memoir. I only hope you've had a fraction of the joy reading about my many adventures in life as I've had living and now re-living them. If I ever write a sequel, you'll be the first to know.

Love, Jerry

EPILOGUE

Since finishing my memoir, I decided that it's time I tackle my iPhone. (Sitting in the box for the past 6 months.) My young friend Anthony who is 17, or a mere 81 years younger than I am, has given me a few lessons. I wish I could say I've been texting and tweeting up a storm but, so far it's not been quite that easy. Frankly, I don't know how the kids do it, especially the two thumbs typing bit.

Anthony giving me iPhone tips

So far, all I've mastered is being able to use Google. Personally, it's staggering to comprehend all the information on the Internet. Among other things, I keep wondering who typed it all. (He or she must be exhausted.)

Thanks to FaceTime, I managed to see Katie's gorgeous new house in Denver. I felt like I was Ed Murrow of the the 1950's TV show "Person to Person" and Katie was my "celebrity star" giving me the grand tour.

And more iPhone "magic," my great niece, Tali, sent me a video of her 2- year-old daughter, Ella singing the ABC's at preschool. It was a joy to behold and I've concluded young Ella, my great-great niece, has inherited the Rosenblum "loving to perform" DNA that my mother passed on to me and my brother, Artie.

Latest addition to the Roberts family, 2019

But the best news from Tali came on August 8th, 2019 when she gave birth to my great-great nephew, with the even "greater" name, Jordan Louis Roberts. I've added a photo of the handsome Roberts family so you can see for yourself.

Meanwhile, I'm happy to report that I wrote a second song for my friend, Congresswoman Alexandria Ocasio-Cortez. I "borrowed" the melody from a 1951 Fred Astaire, Jane Powell, MGM musical, "Royal Wedding." So sweet, AOC actually posted my song on her Instagram page and it got 1,100,050 views in 8 hours! She also wrote such nice notes about me, I almost didn't recognize myself.

The most amazing news was that, on December 21, 2019, I got to meet AOC in person and we chatted for quite a while. (In case you missed it, a photo collage of me and AOC is the second to last of the photos in the middle of the book.) I can honestly say chatting with AOC was one of the happiest days of my life. She's such a genuine person and we really connected. And lastly, there's a possibility, albeit remote because of her incredibly busy schedule, that if/when I do a book signing in New York City, AOC will introduce me!

Thankfully my social life has grown, in large part due to Alice Schultz, my dear friend and companion from my singing class. Often we go to lunch or dinner and recently went to see the movie "Zombieland Double Tap." Why you ask? My dear friend, actress Abbie Breslin co-starred in the movie, and Alice's son, Jim, was the music editor. As it turns out, however, Alice and I are clearly not the demographic for movies about the zombie apocalypse. In fact, at 98, other than Alice, I may have been three times older than anyone else in the whole theater.

Alice and I take a walk in the park, December 2019

Well, that's about it gang. As I say goodbye, I want you to know that writing this memoir has been one of the most gratifying experiences in my long life. The thought that family, friends and total strangers will be reading this and, hopefully, enjoying it, and that possibly AOC may introduce me at a book signing, I almost have to pinch myself to see if I'm dreaming.

IN 50 YEARS IN MEN'S CLOTHING, SOME OF JERRY'S MORE FAMOUS CUSTOMERS

Muhammad Ali (3-time Heavyweight Champion boxer; activist and philanthropist.)

Dick Van Dyke (4-time Emmy-winning actor/comedian)

Robert Merrill (opera singer)

Milton Berle (Emmy-winning performer; Lifetime Achievement Award in Comedy)

Buddy Hackett (actor/comedian)

Vic Damone (singer/actor)

Shirley Jones (Oscar-winning and 4-time Golden Globe nominated actress),

Anthony Quinn (Oscar-winning actor)

Truman Capote (Edgar Allen Poe Award-winning and WGA nominated author.)

Ruth Buzzi (Golden Globe-winning actress/comedian)

Paul Winchell (Grammy winner; ventriloquist; inventor)

Marty Allen (comedian)

Al Haig (General and Secretary of State)

Edmund Muskie (U.S. Senator; presidential nominee)

William Knowland (U.S. Senator CA)

Hubert Humphrey (U.S. Senator, Vice President; Democratic presidential nominee)

John McKethen (Governor of Louisiana)

Tom Bradley (Mayor of Los Angeles from 1973-1993)

U.S. Senator Eugene McCarthy (College professor; politician; poet)

Nguy n Văn Thi u (President South Vietnam)

Kirk Kerkorian (billionaire businessman, investor and philanthropist)

Carl Stokes (Mayor, Cleveland, OH)

Leon Uris (author of "Exodus")

Lee Iacocca (President Ford Motors and Chrysler)

Spiro Agnew (U.S. Vice President forced to resign)

Michael Blumenthal (Secretary of the Treasury)

Mrs. William Scranton (Wife of Governor of Pennsylvania)

Robert Kennedy, Jr. (RFK's son)

Rev. Robert Schuler (Crystal Cathedral, Garden Grove)

David Wolper (3-time Primetime Emmy Award-winning documentarian "Roots")

Dizzy Gillespie (jazz legend)

Barbie Benton (Model/actress/Hugh Hefner's girlfriend)

Abba Eban (Israeli Foreign Minister)

Howard Cosell (sports announcer/ American Sportscaster Hall of Fame inductee, 1993)

Louis Gosset, Jr. (Oscar-winning actor)

Ross Martin (Golden Globe & Emmy-nominated actor: Wild Wild West TV series

Louis Armstrong (Grammy Award-wining musician, orchestra leader; iconic jazz performer)

Mom's Mabley (stand-up comedian)

Jan Pearce (tenor/Metropolitan Opera; Broadway as Tevye in "Fiddler on the Roof" 1971)

Theodore Bickel (Oscar-nominated actor/singer)

Nick Nolte (3-time Oscar-nominated actor)

Robert Young (3-time Emmy Award-winning actor)

Johnny Cash (Grammy Award-winning singer. Country Music Hall of Fame.)

Vincent Minnelli (Oscar-winning director/Liza's father)

Dick Shawn (actor/comedian)

Lanie Kazan (actress/singer)

Stan Freberg (Emmy-winning Actor/legendary TV ad creator)

Al Martino (actor "Godfather"/singer)

Wayne Rogers (Golden Globe-nominated actor "Mash")

Bear Bryant (Alabama University Hall of Fame football coach)

Ara Parsegian (Notre Dame National Championship football coach)

Joe Robbie (owner, Miami Dolphins)

Tommy Lasorda (Hall of Fame manager of LA Dodgers)

Ed "Too Tall" Jones (Hall of Fame Dallas Cowboys football player)

Ken Norton (former heavyweight boxing champion)

Sugar Ray Robinson (Legendary Hall of Fame Boxing Champion)

Jackie Cooper (Oscar nominated and 2-time Emmy-winning actor)

Marie Osmond (singer)

Donny Osmond (singer)

Gladys Knight and the Pips (singers)

Mike Wallace (Golden Globe and Emmy-winning TV journalist; 60 Minutes)

Deacon Jones (Hall of Fame LA Rams football player)

Rev. Billy Graham (preacher)

Dale Roberston (Actor)

Gov. Lester Maddox (Georgia)

Pat Boone (Grammy-winning singer)

Roone Arledge (Created "Wide World of Sports," later head of ABC News Division)

Allan Funt (Candid Camera TV show creator and host)

Minnesota Fats (Professional pool player)

Frank Gifford (Hall of Fame player/Announcer "Monday Night Football" 27 years)

Alan Arkin (Oscar-winning actor)

Edgar Bergen (Oscar recipient of a Lifetime Achievement Award as a ventriloquist)

Della Reese (A Golden Globe and Primetime Emmy nominated actress and singer)

Sir John Mills (Oscar and Golden Globe-winning actor)

Harold Prince (Broadway producer and director and winner of 21 Tony Awards)

Hamilton Jordan (Chief of Staff under President Carter)

Fay Wray (actress: King Kong, Winner of a Special Oscar; born 1907 died 2004!)

Jack Warner (Head of Warner Bros. Movie Studio)

Gary Burgoff (actor, MASH),

Lou Rawls (Singer, songwriter, actor, voice actor, and record producer. 3-time Grammy winner.

Strother Martin (Golden Globe-nominated actor; in Hud: "failure to communicate")

Mills Brothers (singing group)

Sergio Mendes (orchestra leader)

Sterling Silliphant (Oscar Winning screenwriter)

Vic Tanney (Fitness Guru Center),

Pat Buttram (actor/comedian)

Redd Foxx (3-time Emmy Nominee and Golden Globe winning actor/comedian)

Sam Levene (Tony-nominated actor)

Jack La Lane (fitness club owner), Carl Stokes (Mayor of Cincinnati)

Stanley Kramer (six-time Oscar nominated director)

Barney Ross (Boxing Champ in 3 divisions; decorated WWII veteran)

Joel Grey (Oscar, Tony, and Golden Globe-winning actor "Cabaret.")

Ramon Navarro (silent screen actor)

Bonnie Franklin (Two-time Golden Globe and Emmy nominated actress)

Abe Vigoda (Emmy-winning actor)

Rhonda Fleming (actress)

Gene Rayburn (3-time Day Time and 1 Nightime Emmy Nominee game show host)

Jerry West (Hall of Fame Basketball Player with the Lakers)

Alec Baldwin (Oscar-nominated, Golden Globe and Emmy-winning actor)

Don Ameche (Oscar-winning actor)

Paul Moyer (NBC news anchor)

Hal Holbrook (Emmy and Tony-Award winning actor)

Dick Shawn (comedian/actor)

John Payne (actor/writer Writer's Guild of America nominee)

Ted Knight (Two time Primetime EmmyAward-winning actor)

Dick Butkus (Hall of Fame football player)

Louie Nye (Primetime Emmy-nominee actor/comedian)

Anthony Hopkins (Oscar-winning actor and 6-time Golden Globe nominee)

Lawrence Welk (Accordion maestro, orchestra leader, Primetime Emmy TV Show)

Donald O'Connor (Golden Globe and Primetime Emmy-winning actor)

Jennifer Jones (Oscar & Golden Globe-winning actress)

George Romney (former Gov. of Michigan, Mitt's father)

Pat Morita (Oscar, Golden Globe and Emmy Nominated actor "Karate Kid")

Flip Wilson (Golden Globe and Emmy-winning TV comedian)

Bing Crosby (Oscar-winning actor/Grammy Hall of Fame singer)

Karl Malden (Oscar-winning actor)

Greer Garson (Oscar-winning actress)

Sidney Poitier (Director, author, diplomat; Oscar & Golden Globe winner; Honorary Oscar "For extraordinary performances and unique presence on the screen." Cecil B. DeMille Award 1982, Recipient Presidential Medal of Freedom 2009.)

Theodore Bikel (Emmy-winning actor)

Kurt Russell (Golden Globe and Emmy nominated actor)

Goldie Hawn (Oscar and Golden Globe-winning actress.)

Dean Jagger (Oscar and Emmy-wining actor.)

Eddie Albert (2-time Oscar and Golden Globe-nominated actor)

Richard Burton (7-time Oscar nominee, 5-time Golden Globe nominee and 2-time Golden Globe-winning Actor)

Jack Krushen (Oscar-nominated actor)

Glenn Ford (Golden Globe-winning actor.)

ACKNOWLEDGMENTS

First and foremost, I wish to thank my "editor" of this memoir, newspaper columnist Jack Neworth, who was far more than merely an editor. Having spent 50 years in the men's clothing business, I compare the manuscript I originally gave Jack to a bolt of cloth and what he turned it into, to me, was a fine suit. And just like a tailored suit which can take 4 fittings, over many months, this memoir went through 4 drafts until, hopefully, it's ready to be viewed. I am grateful for Jack's patience, talent and, above all, the sense of humor he brought out in my various vignettes.

Next, I wish to thank Catherine Grace O'Connell and Mike Castagna who featured me and Katie as guests on their very popular "Forever Fierce" Podcast. During the hour-long interview I mentioned I was still working on my memoir and O'Connell admonished me, "Dust it off and get it out there! (I hope I got rid of all the dust.)

So many friends and family have encouraged the writing of this memoir, including Dr. Sheila Laffey, who teaches a film class I take at Emeritus College. I wrote a chapter that featured Dr. Laffey who is also an accomplished documentarian.

Many thanks to book jacket designer, Richard Laxlon and photo editor, Ron Heinmiller. Thanks also to Printland Print Center of Santa Monica for their prompt and patient help in printing drafts of the memoir as we progressed to completion.

I also want to acknowledge the work of my multi-talented young friend, Anthony Bvlgari who's going to college soon and has a future that is radiantly bright. He's acted as my PR coordinator graphic designer and technical adviser on all things computer-related.

Above all, I want to thank Katie Miller who's 28 and the best friend anyone could have. On her Instagram page, she describes herself as "the adopted granddaughter of Jerry Rosenblum." Knowing Katie has truly been a privilege and an honor.